CONTENTS

PICASSO

His life

His art

Edited by Domenico Porzio and Marco Valsecchi

Introduction by John Russell

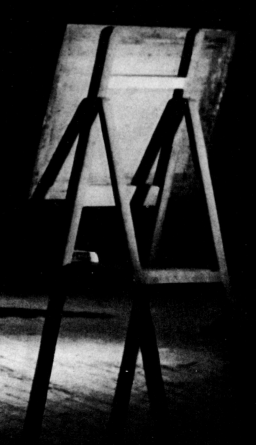

Secker & Warburg
London

TITLE PAGE
Picasso in a frame from the film
The Mystery of Picasso,
directed by Georges-Henri Clouzot, 1955

This edition first published in England 1979 by
Martin Secker & Warburg Limited
54 Poland Street, London W1V 3DF

SBN: 436 37814 0

Graphic design by Daniele Baroni

Printed in Italy

INTRODUCTION

by John Russell

Pablo Picasso made our century his own, in a way not quite paralleled by any other artist. For more people in more places than might have been believed to be possible, he personified modern art. Decade after decade was stamped with his stamp. Even before 1900, at the threshold of the new century, and when he was still in his late teens, he manifested an extraordinary gift for the divination of what people needed to see; and from then onwards, over the next seventy-five years, he was the barometer which generation after generation learned to tap. Inevitably there were ups and downs in his work, and his reputation; inevitably, also, an audience of millions will not respond in the same way as the audience of thirty or forty which was attentive to Picasso at some of the key-moments in his career. But, as with the masterpieces of Old Master painting, there was for everyone who grew up in this century a first sight of *Les Demoiselles d'Avignon*, a first sight of the *Three Musicians,* a first sight of *Guernica* and a first sight of the radiant and euphoric variations on Delacroix's *Femmes d'Alger;* each gave, in turn, a new dimension to the experience of art. These are paintings in which people learned to recognize themselves, and by extension to recognize one another; and we could re-make the list a hundred times over and not come to the end of what Picasso had to give to humanity.

Against all appearances, and in spite of the legend which gained a wider credence year by year, Picasso was in many ways a traditional artist. He retained, that is to say, certain traits which he had brought with him from the century in which he was born. When Picasso first opened his eyes in 1881, Karl Marx and Charles Darwin, Friedrich Nietzsche and Richard Wagner were still alive. They had in common a belief in the supreme powers of the exceptional individual. One man could change the world, as they saw it; and they put that belief into practice. Picasso maintained into the mid-1970s the imperious attitude of mind which prompted *Das Kapital,* and prompted *The Origin of Species,* and prompted *Also Sprach Zarathustra,* and prompted the *Ring.* To the activity of the exceptional individual, no limits need be set: that was the general idea. It was one that had permeated the 19th century; and in his determination to keep working, to get all that could be got from his gifts, and to guarantee the continuity of European achievement Picasso was nearer to the monstrous fertility of Balzac and Victor Hugo than to the short-winded, self-doubting, inter-disciplinary activity which seems likely to characterize the last quarter of our own century.

Picasso was likewise a traditional artist in that he staked a great deal on the exploitation of an outsize personality. When we read how Victor Hugo could break stones with his teeth, and how Monet could pick out a face in a crowd at a hundred yards' distance, we are once again on 19th-century ground. The great man in those days was the man for whom nothing was impossible. The great men of our own century are of another kind – Webern, Kafka, Beckett: masters who turned the 19th century upside down and, shaking it, found all too much that was overblown and self-deceptive. In this debate there was never any doubt where Picasso stood. He might stretch the expressive resources of art in ways undreamed-of before him; but with him it was always a case of one man against life, one man against the limits which should never be set to human experience, one man against the rumoured decline in art's authority. It never occurred to him to substitute the thing thought for the thing done. The artist, for him, was a man who made complete and finite objects and accepted a total responsibility for them. Art was a matter of the eye, the arm, the wrist and the hand; no part of it should be delegated to technology. Picasso to the end of his life made what was fundamentally traditional art – paintings, drawings, prints, sculpture – and he made it for traditional places: the gallery, the drawing-room, the public square. He communicated with his public in ways that Delacroix and Courbet and Manet would have regarded as natural and normal; and in this he was true to the age in which he grew to manhood.

He had, in all this, the most helpful of inheritances. He was the son, that is to say, of a traditional artist who was good but not too good; and he grew up in a milieu – that of Barcelona in the 1890s – which was alert to everything that was going on in art but had not itself produced the kind of overwhelming creative personality which can crush a very young man. The Spanish inheritance in general was not, in this sense, as oppressive as the Italian inheritance. A young man in Rome or Florence in the 1890s might well feel the burden of the past to be so heavy that it was hardly worth trying to be an artist at all; whence the necessity of Futurism. But in Barcelona the case was different. People negotiated both with past and with present as free individuals. We know from the embellished schoolbooks and other juvenilia in the Picasso Museum in Barcelona that Picasso was alive to every work of art that came his way, whether on early visits to the Prado or in the backwater of La Coruña, where his father taught art from 1891 to 1895; but, as with the rest of us, it was above all from his contemporaries that he took his lessons in life.

In this context, several major works of Picasso's early twenties have most often been taken as re-workings of subject-matter then widely current in styles traceable to the masters of the immediate past. Gauguin, van Gogh, and Edvard Munch were domineering presences at the turn of the century and it was inevitable that in addressing himself to tragic subject-matter Picasso should at times echo their work, just as there were lesser artists – Aubrey Beardsley, for one – who entered his awareness, with provocative effect, through the international art-magazines. It has lately become clear, even so, that the great figure-paintings of 1903-05 do not simply derive from that general stock of symbolist images to which any intelligent young painter had access. There is in the pictures in question an intensity of involvement which cannot be explained by the wish – not uncommon among gifted juniors – to go one further than the giants of the immediate past. Picasso was re-living at the deepest level certain experiences which had been fundamental to him: above all, the suicide of his close friend, the painter Carlos Casagemas.

Casagemas had taken his life after a sexual defeat, compounded in his case by the horrors of impotence, at the hands of a woman called Germaine Pichot. (For a full account of this I must refer the reader to Professor Theodore Reff's *Themes of Love and Death in Picasso's Early Work*.) Picasso in adolescence had brought a personal quality even to his re-working in 1897 of so simple-minded a painting as Luke Fildes's *The Doctor;* but after the death of Casagemas in 1901 he revealed himself as a predestined autobiographer – a man who could take the incidents of his own life and raise them to a level of universal significance. It is in this sense that paintings like *Harlequin and his Companion* (1901), *The Kiss* (1903), *The Family of Acrobats with the Monkey* (1903) and, most haunting of all, *The Family of Saltimbanques* (1905) can best be read.

Having and not having are extremes fundamental to the emotional life; and as Picasso himself was nothing if not downright in such matters it is not surprising that the patterns established at the very start of the century should have dominated his art for ever after. Love is possession, or it is nothing: that is the message. Ambiguity is nowhere, gets nowhere, means nothing. Failure is a death-sentence. A woman no longer desired is repulsive. The drama of old age lies in the slow disengagement of man's physical capacities from his still-ardent emotional structure, until he settles at the last for substitutes of a more or less demeaning kind. Like the ritual of the bull-ring to which Picasso was so devoted, this attitude has what a northerner must be allowed to describe as a certain brutal silliness, none the less repugnant for having earned so wide an acceptance. But even if one prefers the alternative tradition – one to which people as different from one another as Titian and George Eliot, Racine and Schubert, may be said to have contributed – it remains true that in paintings like *The Dream* (1932) and *Portrait of Dora Maar* (1937) Picasso gave a new dignity to the notion of ownership in human relations. And as he had, in life, a demonic sense of fun it should also not surprise us that when he painted a portrait into which the question of possession did not enter – the *Hélène Parmelin,* for instance, of 1952 – that sense of fun was given uproarious expression.

In speaking of autobiography, in the context of Picasso's career, I am not thinking of those gravestones of the day-to-day which so many public figures leave behind them. Nor do I mean it in the family-album sense, even if the two portraits of his first wife in this book, and the portrait of his small son Paul dressed as Harlequin, are marvels of undeluded observation. A good autobiography has other and wider echoes. It touches on public events, as they trespass upon the private experience. It touches on the history of sensibility, and it touches on the history of ideas. It remembers Jean-Jacques Rousseau, and it remembers Ruskin's *Praeterita,* and it remembers that least gradiose of Ernest Hemingway's books, *A Moveable Feast,* and it remembers *Les Mots* by Jean-Paul Sartre. In this sense Jacques-Louis David and Eugene Delacroix and Edgar Degas were great autobiographers.

If Picasso is of their number, it is above all for his answers to the question which he pondered all his life long: "What is there still left for art to do?" Only rarely did he tackle public events directly, though I myself would rank the monochromatic *Charnel House* of 1945 as one of the few comments on Dachau and Belsen which measures up to its subject; nor will anyone who was looking at pictures in 1937 and 1938 forget the first impact of *Guernica.* The historian of life in France in the year 1942 should not neglect, either, the still lifes of animals heads – gaunt, dis-fleshed, against a cheerless background – in which Picasso distilled the essence of hunger and enforced passivity.

As for the history of sensibility in our century, it has been to a greater or lesser degree the history of Picasso's own work. But there have been times when he opened himself to climates of feeling which had been set up by others. Through his courtship of, and through his marriage to, Olga Kokhlova he was, for instance, taken into the inmost councils of the Ballets Russes at a time when Diaghilev was trying his hardest to keep the company in being. Now that the entertainments in question can only be recreated in an archaeological spirit we can best approach them, I think, by the study of the drawings and paintings which Picasso made at the time of his involvement: above all, perhaps, by the study of the two versions of the *Three Musicians* which form a monumental postscript to the ballet *Pulcinella*. Faster than almost anyone in the history of art, Picasso could take a new book, a new idea, a new person or a kind of painting not previously known to him and break them down into what could be of use to him and what could be discarded. He did this with surrealism, in the 1920s, in a particularly telling way, and one which was both admired and resented by those who owed surrealism a total allegiance. In dealing with ideas, Picasso was as quick to get out as to get in; and as Michel Leiris pointed out in 1930 Picasso kept in the main to subject-matter that was down to earth and unambiguous and "in any case never borrowed from the hazy world of the dream, nor immediately susceptible of conversion into a symbol: that is to say never remotely surrealist." From the surrealists' point of view, Picasso was both there and not there. It was true that, as André Breton wrote in 1925, "Surrealism has only to pass where Picasso has passed already, and where he will pass again"; but it is also true that at that same time Picasso had been engaged primarily in raising the tradition of classical French still life to a new level of brilliance and festivity. "There and not there": the same may have been said of him by Vladimir Tatlin when he got back to Russia before the Revolution and spoke of the pioneer reliefs which he had seen in Picasso's studio in Paris, or by the sculptors who took note in the late 1920s of how Picasso had opened out sculptural form, or by Henri Matisse when he and Picasso eyed one another's output with a sovereign wariness. But of course there were also times when Picasso was quintessentially "there", with a directness, a vitality and a power of invention which have few parallels in art. One such time began in 1906, when he painted himself holding his palette as an antique warrior held his shield, and went on uninterruptedly till he and Braque said goodbye to one another in August 1914. Looking at the work of those times we remember what Gertrude Stein said: that Picasso was "one who walked in the light and a little ahead of himself, like Raphael". His autobiography, during those years, merged with the autobiography of art itself; and his history was the history of our race at its most vigorous and most inventive. It was as if he had considered the question "What is there still left for art to do?" and returned a one-word answer: "Plenty."

PICASSO
ON PICASSO

CHRONOLOGY

1881   Pablo Ruiz Picasso is born October 26 at Málaga in Andalusia at 36 Pláza de la Merced, the first son of José Ruiz Blasco, a Castilian, and of Maria Picasso Lopez who is of Andalusian origin. His father teaches him to draw and paint at the School of Arts and Crafts of San Telmo.

1891   The family moves to Corunna, a seaport on the Atlantic, where young Pablo continues his early attempts at painting.

1894   The father ceases to paint and gives his brushes and paints to his son, who has demonstrated an extraordinary talent.

1895   The family spends its summer vacation in Málaga and then moves to Barcelona, where Don José has been given a job teaching at the School of Fine Arts which Pablo attends as a student.

1896   The young Picasso rents his first studio on the Calle de la Plata in Barcelona.

1897   The painting *Science and Charity* is given an honorable mention at the National Exhibition of Fine Arts in Madrid. In the autumn, Picasso passes the entrance examination for the advanced course at the Royal Academy of San Fernando in Madrid.

1898   Picasso spends several months with his friend Manuel Pallarès at Horta de San Juan in the Catalan highlands.

1900   The Barcelona review *Joventut* contains the first published drawings by Picasso. He takes his first trip to Paris with his friend Carlos Casagemas. The first International Exhibition is in progress. Picasso sells three drawings to the gallery owner Berthe Weill. He takes over the studio of his countryman Isidro Nonell at 49 Rue Gabrielle. He signs a contract with the art dealer Petrus Mañach who undertakes to pay him 150 francs a month for his entire production of paintings.

1901   In the first part of February Picasso settles in Madrid. He contributes to the founding of the review *Arte Joven;* the first issue comes out on March 31, completely illustrated by Picasso. Starting with this period, the young painter no longer signs his works Pablo Ruiz Picasso but simply Picasso. At the end of March he makes a second journey to Paris. He gives his first show at Vollard's and meets Max Jacob. The Blue Period begins. At the end of December, Picasso returns to Barcelona.

1902   At Berthe Weill's gallery Mañach opens a show of thirty Picasso oils and pastels. In October, Picasso returns to Paris. After staying in various places, he shares a room with Max Jacob on the Boulevard Voltaire.

1903	At the beginning of the year Picasso is in Barcelona. Many of the great haunting canvases of the Blue Period are painted.
1904	Picasso returns to Paris and establishes himself there permanently. He goes to live at the Bateau Lavoir, at 13 Rue Ravignan, now the Place Emile-Goudeau, and remains there for five years. The Blue Period comes to an end.
1905	Picasso meets Guillaume Apollinaire. He acquires a passion for the circus and spends much of his time in the company of actors. During the summer he visits Holland. On his return, he makes the acquaintance of Gertrude and Leo Stein. The Rose Period begins. Fernande Olivier becomes his mistress and he begins his first sculptures.
1906	He meets Matisse, paints the *Portrait of Gertrude Stein*, and spends the summer with Fernande Olivier in Gosol, a small town in the province of Lerida in Spain.
1907	He paints *Les Demoiselles d'Avignon*. He meets Georges Braque through Apollinaire. The dealer Daniel-Henry Kahnweiler, who has a gallery at 28 Rue Vignon, signs a contract with Picasso that gives him exclusive sales rights on his works.
1909	The Analytical Cubism period has begun. The Thannhauser Gallery in Munich organizes a show. Picasso leaves the Bateau Lavoir and establishes himself at 11 Boulevard de Clichy. He spends the summer in Spain, at Horta de San Juan with Pallarès. His first Cubist sculpture dates from that autumn.
1910	He spends the summer at Cadaquès in Spain with Fernande Olivier and André Derain. He paints the Cubist portraits of Ambroise Vollard, Wilhelm Uhde, and Kahnweiler.
1911	Picasso and Fernande Olivier go with Braque and the sculptor Manolo (Hugué) to Céret in the Pyrenees for the summer. He has his first American show at the Photo Secession Gallery of New York.
1912	Picasso meets Marcelle Humbert, whom he calls Eva. They go together to Avignon and Céret, where he works with Braque. He then spends the summer in Vaucluse. The Synthetic Cubism period begins. He makes his first collages, leaves Montmartre, and moves to 242 Boulevard Raspail in the Montparnasse section. He organizes two one-man shows, at the Stanford Gallery in London and at the Dalmau Gallery in Barcelona.
1913	He spends the summer at Céret with Braque, Juan Gris, and Max Jacob.
1914	During the summer, Picasso is in Avignon with Braque and André Derain. His painting *The Jugglers* is sold at the Hotel Drouot for 11,500 francs. When war breaks out, Apollinaire and Braque are called up.
1915	Picasso is living in Paris and painting naturalistic portraits of Max Jacob, Vollard, and others. Marcelle Humbert dies in the autumn.
1917	Jean Cocteau convinces Picasso to collaborate with Diaghilev and the Russian Ballet Company. In February he goes to Rome with Cocteau to design scenes and costumes for *Parade*. In Rome, Picasso meets Stravinsky and the ballerina Olga Koklova, who becomes his wife the following year.
1918	After his marriage to Olga Koklova, he moves to 23 Rue de la Boétie in Paris; he spends the summer at Biarritz.
1919	Picasso goes to London with the Russian Ballet Company. During the summer he works at Saint-Raphael on the Côte d'Azur and paints numerous still lifes.
1920	He spends the summer at Juan-les-Pins. The Neoclassical period begins.
1921	His first son Paul is born. He summers at Fontainebleau.
1922	He spends his summer holidays at Dinard in Brittany. On December 20, *Antigone* by Cocteau is performed in Paris with sets by Picasso.

1923	During the summer Picasso works at Cap d'Antibes and paints a portrait of his mother who has come to visit him.
1924	He designs sets for the ballet *Mercure*, with music by Erik Satie, which is performed in Paris on June 14. During the summer Picasso is at Juan-les-Pins. His large still-life series is begun.
1925	He takes part in the first Surrealist Exhibition at the Pierre Gallery in Paris.
1927	Picasso makes drawings and etchings for an edition of Balzac's *The Unknown Masterpiece* in which the theme of the painter and his model appears for the first time.
1928	The summer is spent in Dinard. After fourteen years, he starts sculpting again.
1930	Picasso summers at Juan-les-Pins. He receives the Carnegie prize for the portrait of his wife, which he painted in 1918. He buys Boisgeloup, a country house near Gisors, in the region of the Eure.
1931	Picasso illustrates the *Metamorphoses* of Ovid with thirty engravings in the Classical style. *The Unknown Masterpiece* is published by Vollard with Picasso's illustrations. An exhibition of "Abstractions of Picasso" is held in New York and a retrospective in London.
1932	The Georges Petit Gallery in Paris presents a large show of his paintings. A similar show is then held in Zurich. The first volume of the immense critical catalogs by Christian Zervos is issued in Paris.
1933	Picasso works this year and the next on the series of engravings commissioned by Vollard, notably the *Sculptor's Studio* and the *Minotaur*.
1934	Picasso makes an extended visit to Spain, including San Sebastiano, Madrid, Toledo, El Escorial, and Barcelona, and paints many bullfight scenes.
1935	Picasso, who is separated from Olga Koklova, begins divorce proceedings that are never concluded. His daughter Maïa is born to Marie-Thérèse Walter. Jaime Sabartès, a friend from his youth, becomes his secretary. He spends a large part of the year at Boisgeloup.
1936	In Spain, he organizes a retrospective show in Barcelona, Bilbao, and Madrid. Picasso spends the summer at Juan-les-Pins and at Mougins in the Alpes-Maritimes. In July, the Spanish Civil War breaks out. Picasso supports the Republican party. He accepts the post of Museum Director of the Prado. Dora Maar becomes Picasso's new mistress.
1937	He makes the two large engravings *Dream and Lie of Franco*. In Paris he rents a studio in an old house at 7 Rue des Grands Augustins and paints the *Guernica* there for the Spanish Pavilion at the Paris World's Fair.
1939	An important show of Picasso's works is held at the Museum of Modern Art in New York. His mother dies in Barcelona. When war breaks out, Picasso leaves Antibes, where he has spent the summer, and goes back to Paris and from there to Royan.
1940	After a period at Royan, he returns to Paris. He is forbidden to show his work during the Nazi occupation of Paris.
1944	After the liberation of Paris, he joins the Communist party. For the first time he takes part in the Salon d'Automne and shows seventy-nine works.
1945	He spends the end of the summer at Golfe Juan. On November 2, he makes his first visit to the shop of the famous Paris printer Fernand Mourlot and starts enthusiastically working at lithography.
1946	Françoise Gilot becomes Picasso's mistress. They spend the summer together at Golfe-Juan and the autumn at Antibes. Picasso presents a series of new and important works

to the Grimaldi Museum. He begins to work with ceramics at Vallauris on the theme of Poussin's *Rape of the Sabines*.

1947   He becomes increasingly absorbed in ceramics and lithography. In May, his son Claude is born to Françoise.

1948   Picasso flies to Poland to take part in the first Communist-sponsored Peace Congress. At the end of the year, a large exhibition of his ceramics is held in Paris.

1949   Françoise Gilot gives birth to a daughter, named Paloma.

1950   Picasso presents his large bronze, *Man Carrying a Sheep,* to town of Vallauris.

1953   Large-scale Picasso exhibitions are held in Lyons, Rome, Milan, Sao Paulo. At the end of the year, Picasso and Françoise Gilot become separated.

1954   Picasso paints a portrait of Jacqueline Roque, who was to become his companion for the rest of his life. He begins series of paintings on the theme of Delacroix's *Women of Algiers*.

1955   He and Jacqueline settle in "La Californie," a large villa above Cannes.

1957   Museum of Modern Art, New York, and the Art Institute of Chicago sponsor large retrospective for Picasso's seventy-fifth birthday.

1958   Picasso executes large mural decoration for UNESCO building, Paris; he buys the Château de Vauvenargues, near Aix-en-Provence.

1961   He moves to the large villa of Notre-Dame-de-Vie at Mougins, a short distance inland from Cannes.

1963   Picasso Museum is inaugurated at Barcelona, due mostly to the efforts of his friend and secretary Sabartès.

1964   Picasso paints a brilliant sequence on the theme of *The Painter at his Easel*.

1966   Grand retrospective show in Paris at the Bibliothèque Nationale celebrates Picasso's eighty-fifth birthday.

1970   Exhibition in Avignon at the Palais des Papes shows all his work from 1960 to 1970.

1971   Picasso does not participate in the festivities of national homage for his ninety years. President Georges Pompidou inaugurates an exhibition of eight canvases at the Louvre. Exhibitions are held at the Grand Palais, the Petit Palais, the Musée d'Art Moderne (the paintings from Russian museums), Paris, and at Lucerne and Vallauris.

1972   Picasso latest drawings are exhibited in December and January of 1973 at the Louise Leiris Gallery (formerly Kahnweiler's).

1973   Picasso dies at Mougins April 8. In December *Seated Woman,* 1909, is sold to an American collector, Sheldon H. Solow, for about $800,000, a record price for a Picasso painting.

THE JOY OF LIVING AND CREATING

by Domenico Porzio

No artist has known in his own lifetime such extensive acclaim as Pablo Picasso, and rarely has such universal homage been bestowed after death. Even veneration for Michelangelo in his old age cannot be compared with that for the aged Spaniard, and the adulation that Rubens's contemporaries gave him was miserly in comparison to that given to the painter of *Guernica*.

Certainly Pablo Picasso has been the most thoroughly discussed genius in the history of Western art. He succeeded in identifying himself and his work with the entire century in which he lived, so much so that the image of our time and our generation will be stamped henceforth with what is depicted in his paintings and sculptures. When France decided to celebrate the artist's eighty-fifth birthday, it seemed that all the great Parisian exhibition halls—the Grand Palais, the Petit Palais, and the Biblothèque Nationale—were scarcely large enough to hold the selection of oil paintings, drawings, ceramics, and sculptures which only partially represented the prodigious production of this tireless protean creator; in terms of the numbers of people they attracted, these exhibitions were an unprecedented phenomenon for Paris.

Miracle Man of the Century

The definitions of the man and the artist are innumerable; they can be chosen from hundreds of metaphors and superlatives found in books, magazines, and newspapers. On the occasion of his death, the chorus of praise mixed with deep sorrow lasted for weeks. The loss was considered irremediable because— it was said—nature requires centuries to produce such a genius and having produced him, will not soon repeat him. Accustomed to considering him immortal while he was still alive, Western culture felt orphaned and deprived. That Picasso was the father and patriarch of modern art is a fact rarely doubted. But admiration for him has changed into fanaticism, almost as if there were something in him more than a painter; it has become a kind of religious identification that goes beyond the virtuosity of his brush and the incomparable and provocative force of his talent. His paintings seem to be outside of

Picasso dons a toreador's cape. Late in life he rediscovered the pleasure of attending bullfights, a rite his father introduced him to as a young boy. "In Málaga, his native town," wrote Ramon Gomez de la Serna, "I understood to what degree [Picasso] is a toreador ... and how, whatever he may do, it is in reality bullfighting."

any accepted aesthetic category, almost as if something might be hidden behind the impetuosity of symbols and colors and beyond the pictorial representation, perhaps a stirring or consoling message, a guide for daily behavior, or even an inspired oracle. In short, the Picasso phenomenon has lasted and still lasts with dimensions that go beyond normal magnitude, as if there were not justification enough in his simply human adventure of being an artist.

The terms and names by which he was measured in his obituary notices do not belong to this century. His supremacy over Matisse, Klee, Mondrian, Duchamp, Chirico, Magritte, and many others who have contributed to the artistic temper of our times has been taken for granted and it seems almost inevitable that he has been compared with Michelangelo. Henry Moore said of Picasso that he was "one of the most naturally gifted artists to appear since Raphael." "For us," wrote André Fermigier in *Le Nouvel Observateur*, "the pleasure that Picasso has given is immense, an unforgettable feast and a performance worthy of the immortals." "Picasso," wrote *L'Express*, "is the supreme injustice: the miracle man whom the cruel gods send to earth once every century to make us believe that a noble life can exist. No one else has been able to survive this century of iron and fire with such a train of glory, liberty and peace. . . ."

The artist's hand mixing colors

The Castle Was about to Fall

Why all this resounding admiration? Why did Picasso please the critics, the masses who flocked to his shows, and those of diverse ideologies? What was his greatness? To know and understand this one must consider all the reasons and truths that contributed to his tumultuous artistic and human adventure. One of the many facts about his "importance" was suspected by the writer Leonardo Sciascia: "The greatness of Picasso does not lie, to state it approximately, in the avant garde, but in tradition. That is, he did not look to the future but to the past, to that which had been done and which he, with his great and feverish talent, could not do again. He could only take apart, break up, and analyze, often with irony, sometimes with disdain, but always with the anger of having arrived when everything had already been done. And thus he went through the whole history of art and art outside history, telling of man and of man's past, reinventing it, remaking it, telling of everything that people today have stupidly denied." Another explanation is the one given by the writer Dino Buzzati: "The old lengendary castle of art was about to fall. He arrived and took possession of it, since it was his house. Being aware of its impending ruin, he hurled his formidable shoulders furiously against the walls. At the same time he lit the fires which started to explode, flash, whirl, and multiply themselves, triumphing in the wonder of everything. Thus no one was aware that, behind the dazzling screen, the palace was little by little disappearing."

Picasso became a myth almost before he was recognized as a great artist, and since this happened too quickly, he was forced to keep the enticing but dangerous myth at bay. Myth and success were the two horns on which he ensnared the black bull of glory: an emotional game for a man who preferred to remain sublimely detached. Around this man, forced for decades to be a kind of living museum, newspapers fabricated a series of Picasso images to satisfy the unconscious myth mania of the public.

The naïve liked the romantic image of the young Spaniard who in his bitter Paris years begged a bowl of soup for himself and his friends and who stayed up at night for hours in front of an easel lit by the fire of a kerosene lamp, an image that reversed itself miraculously when the pauper became a millionaire, a castle owner, a King Midas who transformed everything that he touched with his brush into gold. Others liked the image of the provocative, disconcerting artist who not only destroyed visual objectivity, but also discarded every stylistic conquest almost before he achieved it; who at every exhibition completely changed himself and his work with the apparent indifference of a quick-change artist on the stage, amusing himself by offering a riddle that the critics accepted and always applauded. People liked this clown crowned with glory, this mystic thirsting for a joie de vivre, which was, after all, the joy of painting. To painting he was a slave and faithful servant, capable of dedicating fifteen hours a day, even keeping a supply of paper and pencils beside his bed so that he could draw if he happened to awake. Others liked the great artist who questioned his whole being every day and who worked without complaining of fatigue. Instead, he laughed at it, making life a continuous and joyous work of art interpreted through an inexhaustible and vivacious inventiveness, using a magic wand that no one had given him.

An Example of Freedom

It has been said that Picasso did not create but simply made a seismograph of himself, registering with his hands and as loudly as possible the electrocardiogram of his own feelings, since he had only one person to talk to and account to: Picasso. He often repeated that the problems of painting did not interest him and that he had never worked on nature, only with it. "It is not possible to copy," he said, "even if one really tries. Suppose you want to copy a bullfight, or a Velásquez, or a photograph. You look at it carefully, attentively observing every detail, and finally you possess it. But there is always something that resists you and evades you. What is resisting is you."

In a "Study for Picasso" (in the review *Nous*, 1972), the French writer Claude Roy, who knew him, recounts that he was an artist with modesty, but with an impudently proud modesty. One day, having painted a sad fish that looked like a mullet out of water, he justified himself: "Painting is a thermometer. You put it up your backside and see immediately whether you have a fever or if you're normal." But when he had to respond to an inquiry concerning the greatest living painter, he quoted the bullfighter Garcia, nicknamed Gitano: "They asked him who he thought was the greatest bullfighter of his time. He replied that best of all was Gitano. Then he reflected a moment, and added: 'One could say that Garcia comes immediately after.'"

Anyone who has tried to evaluate Picasso the artist has, in describing his qualities, emphasized his extraordinary freedom and independence, a freedom he lived from day to day that exalted and sometimes frightened those who

Picasso examining some of his engravings: although he often found it painful to exhibit his work, he had helped assemble 201 of his paintings from the years 1970 to 1972 for an exhibition that opened posthumously in May, 1973, at the Palais des Papes, Avignon.

approached him, a freedom that bound him to nothing—neither to what he painted, to the houses he lived in, to the women he loved, nor to the friends who came to visit him. He joined the French Communist party in 1944, but artistically and ideologically he remained a libertarian. And with this same sense of freedom he remained the first nonrealistic painter in the party of Socialist Realism.

One of the definitions that remained with him the longest was that he was the "great rebel," that he always and on everything had a paradoxical and opposite view that astounded others. Notwithstanding his apparent modesty, he felt himself different from others, a trait Guillaume Apollinaire described: "Picasso belongs to the race of those who Michelangelo said deserved the name of eagles, because they surpass all the others and find the day by reaching the light of the sun across the clouds." He loved life with a tremendous and insatiable hunger even if, as Fernande Oliver said, he seemed to have brought to Paris a deep dark sorrow within himself. It was rather the impatience of not being able to live each day to the fullest and of not being able to express daily and uninterruptedly his vast and unique power of creating. In his last years his inevitable thoughts must have been particularly cruel for him—that there was no paradise, even admitting that he had ever suspected one, that could repay him for one day of life and work. He once said to a friend who was surprised to see him breathing fresh air with such passion: "Of course, a day more, a day gained!"

A Religion of Joy

Picasso's personal life is well known from gossip and the several books of memoirs written by the women in his life; and the principal source of information about his early life is the definitive biography by Sir Roland Penrose. His life was not particularly exceptional, despite the seven wives and companions who, judging by his artistic output, did not seem to distract him. The love that dominated his life was his love for what he was doing, a kind of emotional fervor that equalized people and things and nature and ideas on the same plane, that of paper and canvas. The life of Picasso was nothing but a continuous self-preservation so that he could give himself to painting. The very events of his day, which were so cruel and devastating, hardly succeeded in touching him because he considered himself, without presumption, as a fact, an event in history. "If it had not been for *Guernica*," said André Fermigier, "one could have said that he went through two world wars, a time of despair and voyaging to the ends of night, with the indifference of an aristocrat preoccupied only with himself, his own deeds, and his own emotions."

No one could ever reproach Picasso for being a man dedicated to joy as his only religion. But his lack of spiritual pain (aside from participation in and understanding of the pain of others) or of defeat takes away the dimension of suffering and depth from his work. The dramatic quality of his always victorious images lacks that human dimension that vibrates across time in the works of Michelangelo, Rembrandt, Van Gogh, Cézanne, and other greats with whom he has been compared. His happiness, perhaps, was

Examples of Picasso's signature on paintings through 1923: as he became more independent of his family and as he developed his own style, he abbreviated Pablo Ruiz Picasso (at top left from an 1898 watercolor) to simply Picasso, his mother's surname.

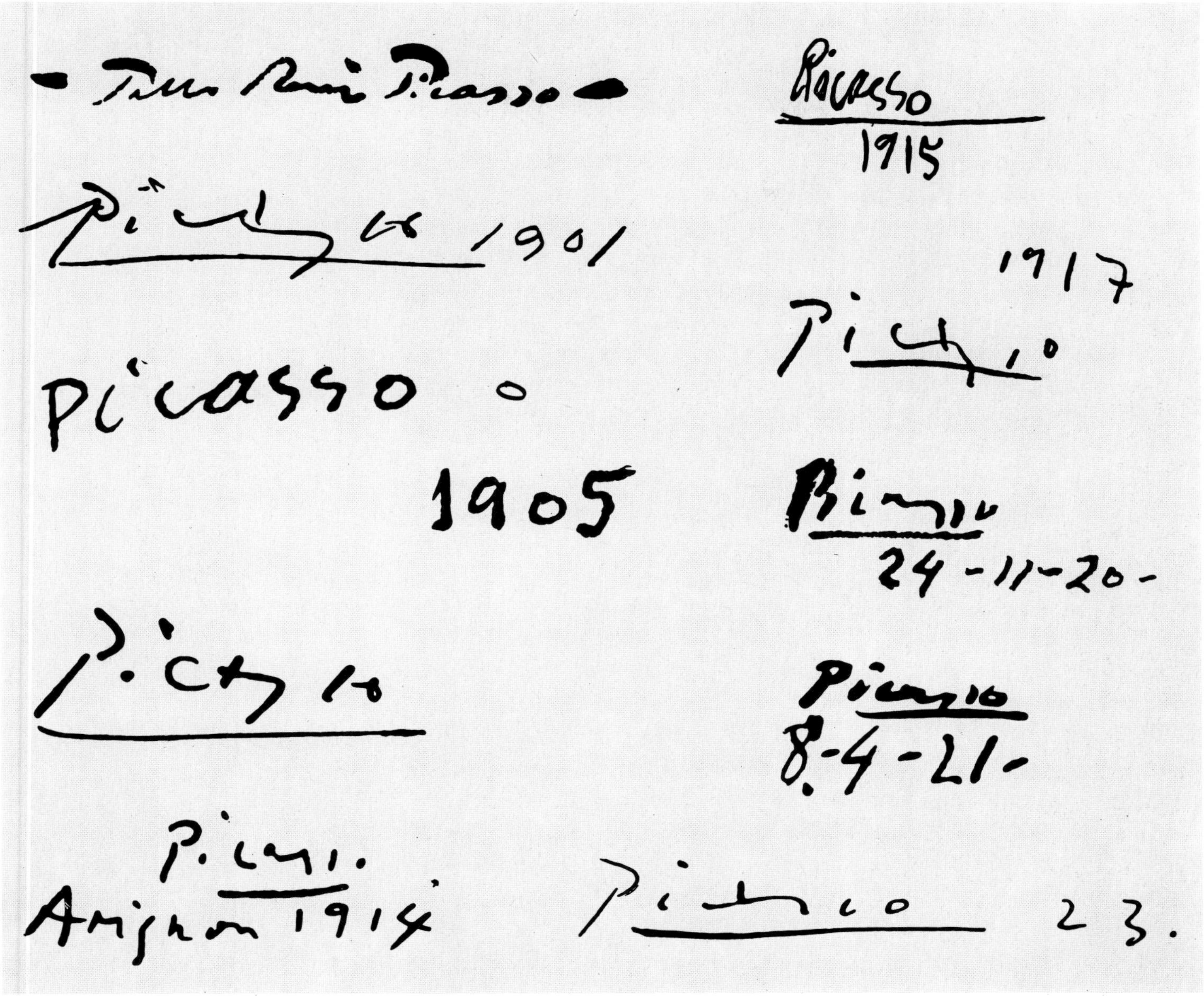

Picasso — Taller Ruiz Picasso —

Picasso 1901

Picasso

1905

Picasso

Picasso
Avignon 1914

Picasso
1915

1917
Picasso

Picasso
24-11-20-

Picasso
8-4-21-

Picasso 23.

exclusively that of intelligence; it germinated inexhaustively within the compass of his ideas. His daily and always surprising world of creativity occurred on a mental level and was the zestful result of a continuous dialectical outburst, rarely served by impulses from the heart or the soul. The reality Picasso reiterated under the guise of revolutionary disaster—which did not exclude his own religious view of life—was a carefully thought-out and programmed reality. What interested him above all else was his completely personal image of the world—divinatory, prophetic, and alarming, to be sure, but nonetheless stemming from an abstraction within which mundane rules of grammar, prosody, and pity naturally have no value. The representation of the universe that he pursued was the one photographed in the camera obscura of his own ego. It was not important to him to see anything directly in the external world. The natural only served as a goad or as a point of departure; and that explains, as Joaquin Mir, a Spanish painter who was almost his contemporary, observed, the almost total lack of landscapes in his otherwise varied production.

The basic problem of any artist, however, is to transmit sensations and ideas into an intelligible and organic order. The painter thus produces something that, by resorting to an intellectual arrangement of objects—that is, by offering a formal rearrangement—appears to most people as a deformation of reality. In Picasso the recourse to deformation was radical and was blown up to the point of annihilation. In this omnipresent principle found in the highest and most eloquent level of his work, however, it is possible to see not only a constant dialectic, but perhaps also the echo of an unconscious and entirely intellectual descent to the lower regions. Disaster is a necessary premise for religious order. In any system of beliefs, including Christianity, the resurgent god mitigates the inevitable tragedy of death, and in Picasso's visionary destructionism one can also detect a transcendental quality.

Exactly at Midnight

The above considerations give some idea of the complexity of the man and the artist. The almost demoniacal naturalness of Picasso's presence in this century and the facility with which he executed his mission of overthrowing and restructuring art subtend his protean personality. Through him an oracular deity seems to have evangelized the history of modern painting, but he was a god with many faces and many arms.

Pablo Picasso was born October 25, 1881, in the city of Málaga, at 15 (now 36) Plaza de la Merced, which is one of the largest squares in the city. According to some he came into the world at a quarter past eleven that night; according to others *a las cinco de la tarde* (five in the afternoon), the traditional hour when, in Spain, the toreadors come into the arena. According to Picasso, the hour of his entry into the world was, as any great apparition would deserve, exactly at midnight.

The Plaza de la Merced was not far from the port and was surrounded by dozens of humble dwellings built of stone taken from the old Moorish city, all inhabited by poor Spanish gypsies. Picasso spoke of his childhood to his lifelong friend Jaime Sabartès, recounting that he was known as a *chupa y tira* ("suck-and-throw"), because the inhabitants of the district ate shellfish almost exclusively and the streets were full of the empty shells they threw from the windows. His father, José Ruiz Blasco, had a relatively distinguished ancestry traceable to a sixteenth-century knight, Juan de Leon, who in 1541 held tax-free possessions in the Valladolid territory and who died in the war between Loxa and Granada. Toward the end of the sixteenth century, the descendants of Juan de Leon left Castile and moved to Córdoba. The appearance of the surname Ruiz in the family is explained by the Spanish custom of adding the surname of the mother to that of the father. In any case, it was in 1790 that a certain José Ruiz de Fuentes, descendant of Juan de Leon, settled in Málaga where he married a woman from the family of Almoguera. His son Diego married Maria de la Paz Blasco y Echevarria in 1830, and they were the grandparents of Picasso. Their first son Diego became a diplomat

Maria Picasso Lopez and José Ruiz Blasco settled in an apartment on the eastern side of the Plaza de la Merced (left, below) when they were married in 1880. Picasso's birth there the following year is commemorated by a plaque over the door of No. 36 (left, above). The birth certificate (above) listed seven Christian names; the first was in honor of his recently deceased Uncle Pablo.

but he gained a certain reputation also as a portrait painter. Another son, Pablo, was a doctor of theology and a canon in the Cathedral of Málaga. He had the task of not only looking after his four maiden sisters but also of helping his younger brother José, the future father of Picasso. José was undisciplined and incapable of dedicating himself to study or to a secure job, so he decided to become a painter.

The maternal surname Picasso was rather unusual but had been known in Málaga for a couple of generations, and it was there that Pablo's maternal grandfather was born. He became a government functionary and died in Cuba of yellow fever. Little is known of the family's origin and there has been much speculation that the name was Italian in origin. Some researchers have tried to establish a relationship between the Picasso of Málaga and the painter Matteo Picasso who was born in Genoa in 1794 and who painted a portrait of the Duchess of Alliera found in Genoa's Gallery of Modern Art. In any case it has been ascertained that the grandfather of Maria Picasso (Pablo's mother) was born near Genoa.

Conjectures and suppositions on the origin of a man of such high destiny as Picasso are inevitable. His friend Jaime Sabartès, for example, has attributed an African origin to him, having discovered in the chronicles of Don Pedro, son of fourteenth-century King Alfonso XI of Castile, a battle between the armies of the King of Andalusia and a certain Prince Picaço, son of the Moorish King Albuhacen, who arrived from Africa with ten thousand cavalry. All this is used to explain the affinity of the painter with nomads and gypsies. "Leaving conjecture and the implications that we hope to deduce from heredity aside," concludes Roland Penrose in his well-known biography *Picasso: His Life and Work*, "it is safe to say that the ancestors of Picasso on both sides are prevalently Andalusian and sufficiently Spanish from sufficiently far back for us to pay attention, above all, to the characteristics of these people."

The marriage between the artist's parents, the painter José Ruiz Blasco and Maria Picasso Lopez, was not coincidental. The Picassos lived in Málaga on the Plaza de la Merced; José, together with his brother Pablo, the canon, lived on the nearby Calle de Granada. The canon insisted that his brother pull himself together and get married (being a painter then was synonymous with being an idler). José thereupon proposed to a young girl who was approved by the family; but he vacillated and finally decided to marry not the designated girl but one of her cousins who had the same surname. The year following the wedding José Ruiz and Maria Picasso had a son whom they baptized in the nearby church of Santiago and on whom they bequeathed the following names: Pablo, Diego, José, Francisco de Paula, Juan Nepomuceno, Maria de los Remedios, Cipriano de la Santisima Trinidad. Pablo, the first name of the series, was a dutiful homage to the canon who had died three years previously.

According to tradition, an error by the midwife almost made the child's birth fatal. It seemed to her that the infant had been stillborn and she abandoned him on a table to assist the mother. Fortunately one of José's brothers, the doctor Don Salvador, was present and saved the newborn infant from imminent asphyxiation.

Millions of Pigeons

Pablo's mother was a small, delicate woman with black hair and black, lively eyes. She always had an unshakable faith in her son, and perhaps it was out of gratitude that Pablo, who resembled her so closely, adopted her surname. His father José was a complete contrast to his wife. He was tall and thin, had reddish blond hair and a reserved and very distinguished appearance. In fact, he was so lacking in vivacity and extroversion that his friends called him "the Englishman."

One of Pablo's first childhood memories was of a December evening, three years after his birth, when Málaga was shaken by an earthquake and a second child, Lola, was born, an event that the painter recalled to Sabartès fifty years later. Don José had decided to take his wife and son to the home of a friend, the painter Muñoz Degrain, because he felt it was more solid. "My mother had her head wrapped in a kerchief—I had never seen her like that before," Pablo recalled. "My father grabbed his cloak from the hook and threw it around his shoulders. Then he picked me up in his arms and wrapped me in its folds leaving only my head sticking out."

With the realization that the profession of an artist did not allow him to meet the ever-increasing needs of his family, Ruiz accepted a post in the School of Arts and Crafts of San Telmo and also became the Director of the City Museum, which was in the Town Hall. To give his wife more space in the tiny apartment in the Plaza de la Merced, he moved his studio to the museum where he had been given a room for restorations. Here he was able to paint undisturbed.

Although he was quite capable, José Ruiz was a limited painter. His specialty was decorative pictures—still lifes with lilacs and feathers, pigeon compositions, and a few landscapes. But for his son he was an excellent teacher. He not only introduced him to the Spanish realist tradition but also taught him to experiment with unusual techniques. For example, he transformed the plaster cast of a Greek goddess into a Madonna of Sorrows by adding false eyelashes and tears of gold and encircling the hair and shoulders with a piece of material dipped in the plaster so that it would stick to the cast. These stratagems—such as using models of pigeons cut out of paper, placing them on the canvas, and moving them about until the exact desired positioning for the composition was found—did not escape the young boy. Thus Pablo learned from his father that to make a picture one doesn't have to be limited to using just brushes and paints but that any material used with patterns, scissors, and paste will do as well.

Doña Maria used to recount that the first word Pablito learned was "piz-piz" to ask for a *lapiz*—a pencil. Once he had it he would scribble for hours. Certainly he learned to draw before he could speak. Like his father, he also soon came to love the pigeons that filled the piazza in front of his house. One picture by his father was indelibly imprinted on his memory. "It was an

Pablo posed for this photograph with his sister Lola when he was seven and she was four. At fourteen he did a pastel of his mother (top) and painted a watercolor of his father (right).

immense canvas," he confided to Sabartès, "picturing a dovecote full of roosting pigeons . . . millions of pigeons." In later years he was to choose the dove as a symbol of peace and of his own ideology. He was also to remember for a long time the bulls and bullfights in the arena of Málaga, to which his father took him as a boy.

Pablo was not yet ten years old when Don José decided to accept a teaching job at the La Guarda Institute, a school in Corunna. He was forced into it out of economic necessity, partially resulting from the birth in 1897 of a second daughter, Conchita, which left him feeling disillusioned and defeated. In 1891, still very discouraged, he set off with his wife and three children for this distant port on the Atlantic coast of Galicia. The isolation from his roots did not agree with him. Corunna was a cold, wintry place without any sun not far from Cape Finisterre. A few months later, Conchita died of diphtheria and he was saddened even further, since she had been the only one of his children who had resembled him.

Corunna was quite an adventure for Pablo, however. The family lived on the Calle Payo Gomez, near the school that Pablo attended, where his father taught. Thanks to his father's position, Pablo enjoyed a great deal of freedom and was able to go to his father's studio and paint and draw rather than stay in class. During this time he perfected his technique in charcoal chiaroscuro. The drawings still in existence are faithful copies of the casts the art school provided. But this boy, who had already been using paints in Málaga, also painted a series of small pictures, including a *Landscape with Farm*, a *Girl Seated*, and a *Group of Boys*. Although he was only eleven years old he began to create art magazines as a pastime, all written and illustrated in his own hand. They were called *Blue and White* and *Corunna* and were filled with street scenes, dogs, babies, and innocent jokes such as the following: "Title: Arithmetic Test. Teacher: If I give you five melons and you eat four of them, how many are left? Pupil: One. Teacher: Be careful you don't get indigestion!"

Naturally he went to secondary school, although it seemed that from morning to night he was entirely absorbed in his drawing. Actually, he had already developed a capacity for work that in time was to become a fundamental and remarkable quality of his life. His genius was of a type that could be called quantitative, but there was no loss in quality, and it is clear that the quantity often ended up turning into quality.

A Solemn Moment

Although he admired and was satisfied with the precocious vocation of his son, Don José was a bit worried about Pablo's studies. The boy had always hated school and had always refused to learn to write correctly, or above all, to learn arithmetic. Sabartès recounts that Don José begged a fellow professor to give his son an exam to teach him something and save him. On this occasion Pablo announced to the examiner that he knew nothing about anything. The teacher vainly tried to get him to write a few numbers in a column. Nothing. He then wrote them on the blackboard and asked the boy to copy them. This was something that the pupil knew how to do very well and so he copied the numbers, imitating the writing of the teacher as if it were a design.

Don José was convinced that Pablo would grow up illiterate, or almost so, and in fact Pablo confessed to his biographer Roland Penrose that he never did memorize the proper sequence of the alphabet. Luckily, his school curriculum was very flexible and the boy was not obliged to amass useless ideas. He would have become, Penrose said, "a frustrated genius with the approved level of scholastic achievement; in fact, an unbalanced and wasted individual." The only satisfaction Don José had in Corunna was the presence of his son in his studio and the enthusiasm with which the boy took to painting.

Pablo would often help him finish his pigeon pictures and still lifes. One evening when Don José was feeling particularly melancholy, he turned the work over to his son and went out for a walk. When he returned the pigeons were finished and were so astonishingly true to life that the father was moved to give Pablo his palette and brushes, with the announcement that his son's talent had now superseded his own and that from then on he would paint no more. It was a solemn moment in 1894; Pablo Picasso was not yet fourteen years old. After this Don José lived only to see his son's success; he was sure Pablo would compensate for his own disillusionment.

The academic teachings of the father had been a strict schooling. They comprised a technical framework that Picasso was never to forget. But at Corunna he had also created imaginative paintings inspired by models of his own choice. His favorite subject was his sister Lola, but there are also portraits of his father's friends and one of Ramon Perez Cortales, a minister in the first Republican government of Spain, who lived near the Ruiz family. The work that the critics most often refer to is a small painting of a barefoot infant girl, *Girl with Bare Feet*, whose hardness of contour, feet and hands show that he was not preoccupied with beauty and that he had a mysterious tendency to depict elephantine forms. This is shown clearly in the paintings of the post-1919 Neoclassical period. Before leaving Corunna the boy reportedly organized a show in a local shop, but he was not able to sell even one of his paintings which today, undoubtedly, would be worth a fortune.

A Prodigy Takes Exams

In the meantime, a post had become vacant in Barcelona at the School of Fine Arts. One of the teachers, a native of Corunna, proposed an exchange of posts with Don José who readily accepted. Before moving to Barcelona, in the summer of 1895, the Ruiz family decided to spend their holidays in Málaga. During the journey they passed through Madrid where Pablo, accompanied by his father, was able to make a quick visit to the Prado and see the works of Velásquez, Zurbarán, and Goya. In Málaga his Uncle Salvador, the doctor who had saved his life as a baby, undertook to encourage his talented nephew. He gave him an allowance of five pesetas a day and a room in an office and even found him a model as well—an old sailor named Salmeron. Pablo did a portrait of Salmeron immediately, but greatly embarrassed his uncle because he had done it so quickly and therefore needed more models.

Picasso at the age of fifteen (top) and eight years later in Paris.

The eager young artist soon painted every relative in sight. Aunt Pepa (top) at first refused to sit for her portrait, but she appeared one August day dressed up in fur coat and fine jewelry. Pablo was called in from play and finished the canvas in an hour. His favorite subject was Lola (above, portrayed in 1899).

The family arrived in Barcelona in the autumn of 1895 and took lodging in the Calle Cristina, not far from the sea and the port, because the School of Fine Arts was only a short distance away. It occupied the upper floors of a huge building called the Casa Lonja, with a courtyard full of fountains and statues.

When Professor Ruiz took his post at the school, his son was fourteen years old and although he had not yet reached the required age he was allowed to take an exam to enter an advanced course. This consisted of drawing from a model and painting, and the time allowed for the examination was one month. Pablo finished it in one day, however, with astounding results.

The drawings, on officially stamped paper, still exist, and they not only reveal an extraordinary technical ability but also an obvious disdain for traditional canons. He drew the muscular and short-legged model with a vulgar and pathetic realism. The professors realized that they were confronted with a prodigy and passed him with full marks.

During his youth in Barcelona, Picasso was slim and lean and had black hair like his mother. He also had his mother's eyes, dark and lustrous with an inexorable hungry look, capable of fixing forever on the retina the faces and things that it encountered, permitting him months later to draw a face or an object as if he had actually made a copy of it.

The Barcelona years (1895–1904) were important for Picasso, not only because he came into contact with an artistic society that was particularly lively and in which he made many stimulating friends, and not only because the surrounding region of Catalonia had many and frequent contacts with French culture, but also because in these years this young man with his tremendous creative abilities succeeded in synthesizing within himself the whole history of art in a panoramic and all-encompassing way. After an undefined period around 1896 he went through a Hellenistic stage when he was from fifteen to seventeen years of age. A Gothic period followed, which lasted until he was nineteen, and finally a Baroque period until he was twenty-one. The last two years of his stay saw the culmination of this mastery out of which the Picasso of Paris was to be born. Picasso's art was always characterized as a passage from one stylistic conquest to a loss of faith in the conquest just achieved —not a progression, then, of successive additions, but rather advancement through a series of destructions. "I make a painting," he once said, "and then I destroy it. But nothing is lost. The red destroyed in one place turns up in another."

First Steps to Personal Freedom

Soon after the exam the family moved to a more comfortable house on the Calle de la Merced, No. 3, and Don José found a studio in the nearby Calle de la Plata where his son, now a student at the School of Fine Arts, could work. Here Pablo painted a work, which has since disappeared, called *Bayonet Attack,* and soon after, a painting which was not lost because his sister Lola kept it in her house as long as she lived. It was entitled *Science and Charity.* His father posed as a model for a doctor who is feeling the pulse of a woman lying in bed, on the far side of which is a nun who is handing a cup to the sick person and at the same time holding a baby. It is a completely academic work and was given an honorable mention at the National Exhibition of Fine Arts at Madrid the next year and a gold medal in Málaga.

Then, still following the advice of his father, he painted, among many others, a picture with the subject *The First Communion*. This also ended up in his sister's house. Between his sixteenth and seventeenth years the young man worked feverishly, as always, trying whenever he could to rebel against the academic style that had been imposed on him and attempting to find something personal. To this end a painting from 1897, a small sketch of the interior of a tavern, was important. It shows a smoky room lit by a tiny window, against which are silhouetted groups of figures. It conveys the sensation that Picasso might have seen reproductions by Daumier and suggests the early Van Gogh. In the summer of that same year he went with his family to Málaga. Here he had a romance with his cousin, Carmen Blasco, and his Uncle Salvador hoped that the young man would settle down in Málaga to the honor of the family; but at the time he flaunted his independence with a showy black hat and a stick in the manner of students in Catalonia.

He disappointed his family when in October he returned with his father to Barcelona and forgot Carmen immediately. In the following winter Pablo moved to Madrid to attend the Royal Academy of San Fernando. Since in order to register he had to give samples of his work, he repeated his Barcelona performance in the capital. In a single day he finished all of the drawings required and thus at sixteen years of age passed all the academic tests required in Spain by the official schools.

He found himself modest lodgings, but he realized that it would not make any sense for him to attend the academy. He preferred to spend long hours at the Prado and at work on his own projects. This behavior did not please his relatives who expected him to be a traditional painter, and the fact that Pablo did not attend the academy seemed like a betrayal. His Uncle Salvador had promised to send a monthly allowance but he decided not to send any more money. Since what his father sent was very little, the young man started to experience the pangs of poverty. Nevertheless he suffered it happily in order to be able to do what he wanted and to enjoy complete freedom. In the spring, however, he became ill with scarlet fever and in June was forced to return to Barcelona. Here a friend, Manuel Pallarès, also a painter, proposed a joint trip to Aragon, to his native village of Horta (meaning garden) de San Juan, now called Horta de Ebro, and Pablo accepted.

The countryside was a revelation to him and it remained in his memory for a long time. In his Cubist period it gave him the inspiration for some of his rare landscapes. The country was bathed in strong color and the peasants' struggle against nature was a hard one. He also wanted to learn how to farm, fascinated as he was by all aspects of the tasks, even the most humble ones, connected with it. Later he was to say: "Everything that I know I learned at Horta de San Juan."

It was there that he acquired a complete psychological freedom and

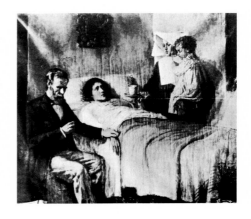

Science and Charity (top), painted in Picasso's first studio, won an honorable mention (above) at the 1897 National Exhibition of Fine Arts in Madrid. Don José, who had chosen the subject, was able to keep an eye on the work's progress by serving as the model for the doctor in the foreground.

Jaime Sabartès, a Catalan poet, first met Picasso on a narrow Barcelona street in 1899. Their friendship was cemented in 1935 when the solitary painter asked Sabartès to join him in Paris. "Since that day," Sabartès wrote, "my life followed in the wake of his." The 1901-1902 portrait at right was one of the first of many. Sabartès was a main founder of the Picasso Museum, Barcelona; he donated 427 works given to him by Picasso.

strength of character. In the village he made many drawings and even a few paintings. He also met a young girl and fell in love. She was the Joceta Sebastia Mendra who posed for *Head of a Young Girl* dated November, 1898.

Picasso remained in Aragon long after he had recovered from his fever, living in the hottest months with his friend in a mountain cave, happy to be isolated and to be able to draw what pleased him. The sketches from this period, especially those of animals, are quite remarkable.

The Four Cats

In the early spring of 1899, Pablo returned to Barcelona where he met Jaime Sabartès, who was to be his faithful friend for the rest of his life. They met, Sabartès relates, at No. 1 Calle de Escudillero Blanco, where Picasso was using a room in a friend's apartment as a studio. In this room he had stored all his paintings, including those painted at Horta. He was about to enter that period which has since been defined as the Modernist period and which

A bohemian beer hall known as Els Quatre Gats had been established in Barcelona to imitate the intellectual life of a Parisian cabaret when Picasso returned there in 1899. He was soon a frequent habitué, painting posters (below) and sketches of the clientèle (Ricardo Opisso and Sabartès, right center). Other works of this period were *Le Divan* (right) and a dancer (bottom left). His first exhibition was hosted by the café in 1900.

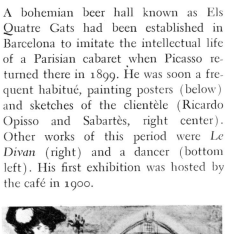

The Catalan modernist movement, centered in Barcelona, tried to expand its influence through literary periodicals, for which Picasso became an illustrator. His first published drawing (top) appeared in the July, 1900, issue of *Joventut*; *La Boja* (left) accompanied a story in *Cataluna Artistica*. Picasso's name is plainly visible on a drawing (above) in the Barcelona *El Liberal*.

had as its focus a beer hall known as Els Quatre Gats (the Four Cats) which had been opened by Père Romeu. This man, who was a seasoned traveler with a spirited personality, opened his premises on the model of the Parisian Chat Noir, with the idea of making it a meeting place for intellectuals. He provided a tavern, an exhibition hall, and a room for concerts and the marionette theatre of Miguel Utrillo, the adoptive father of the French Impressionist painter Maurice Utrillo.

The painter Ramon Casas and the elder Utrillo also published two art periodicals and organized shows in which Isidro Nonell, Santiago Rusiñol, and the Basque painter Zuloaga participated. When the Four Cats was inaugurated, Picasso was in Madrid but once he returned to Barcelona after his vacation in Aragon he immediately became a regular customer and favored guest. He drew a series of caricatures of his friends which were hung on the wall; he took part in reunions and meetings; and he made a poster and a menu for the tavern in a style that faintly resembled Japanese prints and whose tenuous colors, with thick black outlines, resembled Gothic stained-glass windows. In this period, which was full of effervescence and rich with acquaintances, he did, among other things, a pastel entitled *Mother and Child*, which seems inspired by William Blake, a *Rose Branch* in an extremely floral and decorative style, and a series of *Scenes of Bohemian Life*.

His first published drawing was one that appeared in the review *Joventut*. It was a charcoal drawing of a female figure with bare breasts, used to illustrate a Symbolist poem by Joan Oliva Bridgman called "The Call of the Virgins." The design is full of Nordic symbolism, like the one he did for another poem by the same author, "To Be or Not to Be," and the illustration *La Boja* (the mad woman) for the story by Surinac Senties.

Barcelona was also full of German influences. Nineteen hundred was the city's year for Wagner and both *Tristan und Isolde* and *Siegfried* were performed. The magazines translated numerous German authors, evoking German mythology and presenting texts by Schopenhauer and Nietzsche—the two idols of the moment—as well as reproductions of paintings by the Swiss Arnold Böcklin.

Discovery of Paris

Pablo felt more and more the need to get away; even his Barcelona experience had become an exhausted curiosity. When Miguel Utrillo, Rusiñol, and Casas returned from their trips to Paris they spoke of a fabulous city with important galleries, extraordinary museums, and a lively and fascinating culture. In these months Picasso had become the friend of the young painter Carlos Casagemas, a tall, thin man with a receding chin and pointed nose, as the many caricatures of him show. Pablo shared his third Barcelona studio with him on the Calle Riera de San Juan, an austere studio with white walls that he frescoed, painting on the walls all the commodities their poverty forced them to do without. But in October of 1900, the two friends decided to set off north in search of new adventures. Their goal was London and England, because Casagemas loved the Pre-Raphaelite painters and harbored romantic notions about English women as being full of character and courage as well as being very beautiful. Paris was an obligatory stop on the projected trip. Pablo arrived with Casagemas in the French capital a few days after his nineteenth birthday. They rented Nonell's former studio at 49 Rue Gabrielle and proceeded to visit theaters, cafés, and the Louvre and other museums. They saw the paintings of Degas, Van Gogh, Gauguin, and Toulouse-Lautrec. Picasso also visited Mlle. Berthe Weill who owned a little gallery and eventually became Matisse's first dealer. In the gallery he chanced to meet a Catalan industrialist, Petrus Mañach, who had begun to be interested in becoming a dealer in drawings. Mañach made a contract with him of 150 francs for his entire monthly production and at the same time Berthe Weill paid one hundred francs for three paintings of bullfights that Pablo had brought with him.

As a result of these transactions, Picasso considered himself independent and knew he did not have to return to Barcelona until he wanted to. In Paris he painted and did a number of drawings. In these and in the painting *Le Moulin de la Galette* (Plate 2), the influence of Toulouse-Lautrec is strong. In December, for Christmas, the two friends decided to return to Spain. Casagemas had experienced an unhappy love affair in Paris. Pablo thought that a return to Málaga would be good for him, but everything went badly.

When the two friends arrived in Málaga with their long hair and shabby clothes, they were at first refused lodgings at the inn of the *Tres Naciones* and Picasso was forced to call upon a paternal aunt to guarantee the bill. When Uncle Salvador saw his nephew with such eccentric behavior and clothing he became disgusted. Even his father Don José drew away from his son, realizing that Pablo no longer needed him or his teaching. After a few days Pablo went off to Madrid and Casagemas returned to Paris where he committed suicide with a pistol in a café (see Plate 4, *Burial of Casagemas*).

When Pablo arrived in the capital he met a friend from Barcelona, Francisco Soler, who talked him into becoming his associate on the review *Arte Joven* which was about to be launched. Soler was the Madrid representative for a miraculous electric belt which had been invented by his father to cure all ills. He was trying to start the review with the earnings from his sales. Five numbers were issued with drawings—self-portraits and Parisian sketches —by Picasso.

After this interval Pablo returned to Barcelona to see friends; they threw huge parties for him and invited him to take part in a show at the Sala Parès. There he exhibited a few of his pastels and in these the influence of Degas, as well as Toulouse-Lautrec, was evident. It is important that for the first time the works were signed Picasso, and in fact it was on this occasion that he decided to adopt the single surname of his mother.

"Only Love Counts"

Picasso's second journey to Paris was in 1901. His dealer, Mañach, awaited him impatiently—he had even rented a studio for him on the Boulevard de

On Picasso's first visit to Paris in 1900 he met Petrus Mañach (top right) who gave him a monthly stipend. Mañach was not very pleased, however, with the subsequent output of Picasso's Blue Period, typified by *The Tragedy*, 1903 (bottom right). *End of the Act* (top) and *Self-Portrait*, 1901 (above), were painted during his second visit when he met Max Jacob, to whom the 1904 *Self-Portrait* (center right) was dedicated.

Clichy, the room that Pablo painted in the picture *The Blue Room*. A little later, Mañach introduced his young friend to the dealer Ambroise Vollard, who ran a gallery on the Rue Lafitte. "In 1901," Vollard wrote later, "a rather elegant young Spaniard came to visit me. It was Picasso. He was about twenty years old and had completed a hundred paintings which he brought to me for an exhibition. The show was not a bit successful and it was some time before Picasso was to receive a more favorable reception from the public."

It was then that Pablo met the painter, poet, and critic Max Jacob and a friendship was begun between the two that ended only with the death of Jacob in a Nazi concentration camp. In the winter of 1902 Picasso returned to Barcelona where he worked in a studio on the Calle del Conde del Asalto until the following October. Mañach was not happy with what the painter was now turning out—no more café scenes and lighted streets, but emaciated and despairing figures (Plates 5 and 6). In the meantime Vollard was having a second show, and Picasso visited Paris a third time with Sebastian Junyer-Vidal. After staying in a miserable attic in the Hôtel de Maroc, he rented a room with Max Jacob on the Boulevard Voltaire. It was a cold and bitter winter and the two men, in complete poverty, could not keep warm. In a moment of desperation Picasso stuffed the stove with pastels and drawings he had done in Barcelona and Paris and burned them. They arranged their life together so that the bed was always occupied. By night Max slept in it and Pablo worked; by day, their roles were reversed.

About six months later, Picasso returned to Barcelona, but he did not forget his association with Max Jacob and he wrote him long, sad letters. This was a period of great restlessness as well as poverty. His contract with Mañach was finished, and he was in search of a new sculpturesque style. In these months he lived the drama of loneliness; he wrote to Max Jacob that he needed to "do something." This stay in Spain lasted for more than a year and is memorable because it saw the birth of some of the most beautiful paintings of the Blue Period: *The Sarto Soler Family Group*, *Life*, *The Old Guitarist* (Plate 12), *Woman with Arms Crossed*, and *The Blind Man's Meal*. It was perhaps the first truly elevated and decisive moment in the life of the man and in the evolution of the artist. The theme of sky, full of pathos, was used insistently. He had said the year before: "It is only love that counts." To this phrase, which he often repeated, he now added: "They should take away an artist's eyes, as they do to goldfinches to make them sing better."

The solitude that had seemed a curse soon became a style of life that he maintained even when he lived in huge villas with several children, dogs, and servants. "It is impossible to do anything without solitude," he declared, "and I have created a solitude for myself that no one suspects."

At a little more than twenty years of age he already had to his credit an immense body of work, more than a thousand paintings, drawings, and engravings, even though a large part of it was academic. Yet the early work was only a fraction of his eventual output of at least fifteen thousand titles.

In the first months of 1904 he moved to another studio in Barcelona on the Calle del Commercio, to have more space and greater freedom. The isolation gave a new impetus to his creative capacities. Sabartès recounts that one day Picasso came to visit him in the house where he lived near his studio and decorated the walls "in the spirit of Assyrian bas-reliefs." But he did not really succeed in finding himself in Barcelona, so in April of 1904 he went off to Paris, leaving Catalonia forever.

Love and Poverty in Paris

The Bateau Lavoir in Paris is a tenement house baptized thus by Max Jacob because it resembled the laundry boats along the Seine. The building was situated on a small square which is now called the Place Emile-Goudeau. It was old, run-down, and had no water or plumbing. It was where Gauguin and the Symbolists had lived and Picasso installed himself there for the next five years. Something, he knew, had to happen to his painting.

The Bateau Lavoir was almost uninhabitable. In the winter months it was open to the winds and the cold, and in the summer it became a fiery oven. It was here that Picasso met his first mistress, the beautiful Fernande Olivier, who was a student at the Ecole des Beaux Arts and a friend of many of the painters. Picasso had frequently run across Fernande at the dwelling but they never spoke to each other. One summer's day, a sudden rainstorm forced Fernande, who was in the square, to take refuge in the entrance hall where Picasso was standing.

"He had a kitten in his arms," she wrote in her memoirs, "and at the same time, laughing and blocking my way, he made a pass at me. I laughed and he invited me to see his studio."

Fernande described the Picasso of this period as a small dark man, poorly dressed and disheveled: "At first glance, there was nothing attractive

Among the tenants sharing the dubious comforts of the Bateau Lavoir (left) was Fernande Olivier whom Picasso engaged in conversation and invited to his studio soon after he moved in. "La belle Fernande" relieved some of the sorrow of his life; rose began replacing blue as the dominant color on his canvases. His relationship with Fernande (right) lasted for six years, until 1912.

about him. But his eyes! His penetrating look attracted the attention of everyone. Socially it was difficult to place him, but this radiance, this internal fire that one felt in him generated a kind of magnetism, which I could not resist."

Picasso was respected among the young painters of Montmartre and writers often came to his aid: Max Jacob, the critic André Salmon, Pierre MacOrlan, and Guillaume Apollinaire, the poet and standard-bearer of modern art. Notwithstanding this, and in spite of the fact that he even sold a few paintings, Pablo and Fernande went through a period of abject poverty. When he chanced to sell something to a secondhand bric-a-brac dealer, Père Soulier, he was lucky to get twenty francs for ten drawings. He had established a connection with Vollard, but he had no exhibitions, partly because he was not much interested in organizing them. His circle of friends widened and his studio began to be frequented by Spanish and French artists: Matisse visited him, as did Georges Braque, Raoul Dufy, Marie Laurencin, Utrillo, Jean Paul Laurens, Lipchitz, and Marcoussis, as well as the writers Cocteau and Apollinaire.

"The presence of Apollinaire," Sabartès has written, "was important because he was cultivated, intelligent and imaginative—three qualities which were essential for the atmosphere surrounding Picasso and which were indispensable elements for the intellectual revolution which was in preparation." Apollinaire, in fact, was one of Picasso's prophets. Already in 1905 he had written his first article on him.

These were hard but happy years, with evenings spent in long conversation with friends and every now and again a night spent at the Lapin Agile, a small café. Pablo worked frenetically, almost always at night. In 1905 he took a short trip to Holland but did not bring back any particular impressions from it. At the Bateau Lavoir he tried sculpture as well, with the

help of Fernande, and it was here that he met Gertrude Stein whose brother Leo had begun to buy some of his paintings and had become his friend. It was then that Picasso painted his acrobat series (Plates 14, 18, and 19) and Vollard, who was visiting him one day in his studio, bought thirty paintings for two thousand francs. For Pablo and Fernande it was a huge sum and they decided to take a trip to Spain.

They spent the summer of 1906 in Gosol, in the province of Lerida. The holiday was interrupted by a typhus epidemic in the area and an alarmed Picasso wanted to return to France at all costs. A few months before, he had finished the portrait of Gertrude Stein (Plate 26). The American writer was forced to sit eighty times for the painter without much result. Picasso succeeded in finishing the picture by painting Gertrude's face from memory. A friend expressed some criticism on the resemblance: "Don't worry," Picasso replied, "she'll end up looking just like that."

After the summer at Gosol his paintings underwent an important change. In the pictures done in Spain, the human figure has a statuesque quality, with simple and heavy modeling, a notable example of which is *La Toilette* (Plate 24). These are the last examples of the Rose Period. The year 1907 and the big switch to Cubism were about to begin.

Collaborators in Cubism

Les Demoiselles d'Avignon (Plate 30), the picture that inaugurated Cubism, dates from 1907. It was a tour de force. When his friends saw it, nearly all of them shook their heads, even Apollinaire. He reproved Picasso for his "philosophical brothel" of nudes. Manet, Goya, and Van Gogh had already maltreated the human figure, but no one had dared go quite so far. This new Picasso painting destroyed a whole figurative tradition. André Salmon wrote: "Here problems are laid bare. White ciphers on a blackboard. The principle of painting is proposed as an equation." The painting "inaugurated modern art by modifying the nature of the relationship between the painted image and reality and by thus placing the person who looks at it in a position he has never before occupied," said Jean Luis Ferrier.

In 1909 Picasso left the Bateau Lavoir to move to 11 Boulevard de Clichy. During the summer he returned to the Spanish village of Horta de San Juan in Tarragona, where he had been ten years before, to stay with his old friend Pallarès. There, taking off from Cézanne, he painted the austere landscape and clusters of houses in geometrically defined planes and reduction of color that further announced the advent of Cubism (Plate 35). There followed that winter the Cubist portraits of the dealers Daniel-Henry Kahnweiler, Wilhelm Uhde, and Ambroise Vollard (Plate 42). The latter recounts how everyone who entered the studio and saw the painting asked what it was: "But when the five-year-old son of a friend of mine saw it, he raised his finger and said: 'Look it's Vollard!' "

During this time Picasso was in close touch with a group of artists in Paris that included Braque, André Derain, and Matisse, the latter of whom he met frequently at the Steins. But it was with Braque that he was partic-

Paris was Picasso's home and artistic base from 1904 until the late 1940s, although he never gave up his Spanish citizenship. He posed in Braque's French soldier's uniform in 1909 (top left), a year increasing prosperity enabled him to move with Fernande to an apartment on the Boulevard de Clichy (center left). His Analytical Cubism period was at its height a year later when he depicted ˋ Daniel-Henry ˙ Kahnweiler (right). The young dealer sat more than twenty times for the portrait; he was one of the first to champion Picasso's extraordinary transformation of pictorial vision. In the summer of 1912 Picasso moved to Montparnasse with Marcelle Humbert. He is shown in his studio (bottom left) in 1915, the year she died.

ularly close, and there grew between them an intimate colloquy that amounted to actual collaboration in the development of Cubism. The summer of 1911 they spent together at Céret, in the Pyrenees, during which time and after their return to Paris they spent hours discussing and sharing their views on this radical transformation of reality. So close are some of their works that Braque once admitted "we had difficulty recognizing our own paintings."

Of the new development, Picasso felt compelled to write: "Many people think that Cubism is a kind of transitional art or an experiment which will mature and be capable of producing different results. They are the ones who have not understood Cubism. It is simply an art which is concerned with form—and when a form is created, it exists and lives its own life."

In 1912 Picasso met Marcelle Humbert who was a friend of Fernande's and mistress of the sculptor Marcoussis. It was love at first sight. Picasso ran off with Marcelle and said good-bye forever to Montmartre. Marcelle was Eve for him—he called her Eva—and the inspiration for a series of beautiful

39

paintings. He was disgusted with the poverty-stricken life that he had hitherto led, and after a trip to Provence he moved with Eva to 242 Boulevard Raspail. Here he began a series of collages and experimented with new techniques, always in search of new solutions. In the summer of 1913 Picasso returned to Céret, along with Juan Gris, Braque, Manolo, and Max Jacob. Perhaps stimulated by the new freedom of collage, color began to reappear in his paintings, after the rigor of the initial analysis of form.

In the meantime Kahnweiler offered him an advantageous contract. At thirty-three years of age he was a famous and well-paid man; in the spring of 1914 his painting *The Jugglers* was sold at an auction at the Hôtel Drouot for 11,500 francs. But it was also a rather sad time. His father José Ruiz had died a year earlier; the onset of World War I broke up the close association of the Cubists; and Marcelle Humbert died in the fall of 1915.

Marriage and Convulsive Beauty

When war was declared many of Picasso's friends left for the front. Apollinaire enlisted, was wounded in the head, and died from pneumonia in 1918. Braque left and he also suffered a head wound. Picasso was staying in a studio on Rue Schoelcher, in Montparnasse. He was to all intents and purposes alone; even Max Jacob in this period had abandoned him. He then moved to 22 Rue Victor Hugo. It was in 1917 that Cocteau visited him to ask if he would like to work on set designs for Serge Diaghilev's Russian Ballet. Picasso accepted immediately, but his Cubist friends accused him of betrayal.

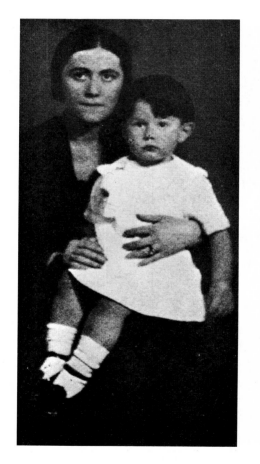

In February he went with Cocteau to Rome to design the costumes for Cocteau and Erik Satie's ballet production, *Parade*. In Rome Pablo met the ballerina Olga Koklova (Plates 62, 63) who in July left the company to follow the painter to Spain. They were married the following year with Cocteau as the witness at the wedding. The collaboration with the Russian Ballet continued until 1924. Picasso designed the scenery and costumes for *The Three-cornered Hat* by De Falla and, in 1920, for Stravinsky's *Pulcinella*, displaying, as the latter composer once wrote, an extraordinary sense of theater. In these years, he and Olga spent their summers at the Cap d'Antibes, at Juan-les-Pins, and in Cannes—they were happy years. In 1921 his son Paul was born and the family went to live in the Rue de la Boétie, in a house whose interior he depicted many times.

In 1924 the Surrealist movement became influential, led by André Breton, and Picasso participated in the first Surrealist Exhibition, which opened in 1925 at the Pierre Gallery. Besides Breton, the new men he befriended included the writers Paul Eluard, Louis Aragon, and Robert Desnos, and the painters Max Ernst, Joan Miró, and Man Ray. This period ushered in a rapid change of style in his work.

"My many styles," he declared, "should not be considered as phases in an evolution . . . I have never made banal experiments. Every time I have had something to say, I have said it in the way in which I felt it should have been said. Different subjects require a different mode of expression."

40

A letter contract with Kahnweiler (left) and marriage to Olga Koklova (with their only child Paul, left, below) contributed to making Picasso's lifestyle remarkably bourgeois. In a 1929 photo (right), he is wearing an atypical homburg, dark tie and suit. Two years later he bought a country house in Boisgeloup (below), which he eventually gave to Olga. They were separated in 1935, the year Picasso's daughter Maïa was born to Marie-Thérèse Walter (bottom).

He was most fascinated with the Surrealism of Breton, according to whom "beauty must be convulsive or cease to be." This fascination coincided with his desire to find a more dynamic mode of expression. In 1925 he painted *Three Dancers* (Plate 83), a convulsed configuration with a frenzied deformation within, testimony to his need to express furor and inaugurating the period of "monsters" which were to remain for a long time in his work.

While this proclaimed a profound break with the Neoclassicism of his theater designs, Picasso during the next few years was to strike out simultaneously in other new directions. In 1926 appeared his notorious *Guitar* of cloth, paper, string, nails, and oil on canvas. Then in 1927 he was to devote himself to the semiabstract and other drawings to illustrate Balzac's *The Unknown Masterpiece* (published by Vollard in 1931). Finally, obsessed with the idea of invoking pure volume conceived as sculpture during the summer of 1928 at Dinard, he filled his notebooks with drawings preceding the monumental series of *Bathers*, shocking in their fantastic semiabstraction, dating from 1928 to 1937 (Plates 99, 100).

In 1928, after a break of many years, Picasso also returned to sculpture. Three years later he received an award from the Carnegie Foundation and bought himself the château of Boisegeloup, a country house south of Gisors. His marriage to Olga was beginning to fall apart. It had lasted seventeen years and in 1935, after divorce proceedings which were never properly concluded, Picasso left his wife. In reality, a new woman had entered his life, the German model Marie-Thérèse Walter who gave birth to his daughter Maïa (Maria de la Concepcion) in 1935.

From Guernica to the Occupation of Paris

In 1936, civil war broke out in Spain and Picasso was invited to become the Director of the Prado in Madrid. Obviously he took the side of the Republicans and drew and wrote against Franco. His relationship with Marie-Thérèse continued for several years—he often visited her and his daughter at their Paris apartment—but in 1936 he also met Dora Maar (Markovitch), a Yugoslavian photographer who became his mistress. She remained with him for ten years and was the inspiration for several portraits that are among the most beautiful Picasso ever painted of a woman (Plate 97). He then settled into a new studio at 7 Rue des Grands-Augustins, an enormous studio where he painted *Guernica*, his most celebrated picture (see foldout facing page 73).

The theme for this work was suggested by the indignation felt over the indiscriminate and brutal bombing of the little village of Guernica. In Picasso's huge graphic apocalypse, all the motifs of distortion and monsters painted in the preceding years are brought into play to produce a human and civic indictment of the horrors of war. To Picasso, who was then fifty-six, destiny had provided the opportunity for a grand subject. The picture is an allegory of violence and beauty and is probably his best-known work. And yet when it was displayed in Paris in June, 1937, at the Spanish Pavilion of the World's Fair, there were moralists who asked that it be removed because it was "unworthy of the mental health of the proletariat."

This was not the first time that the world of officialdom had mistreated the talented artist. After World War I a deputy had requested that Picasso be refused permission to exhibit in French museums.

In 1939, the year that World War II broke out, Picasso was particularly unhappy. For a long time he had suffered a serious form of sciatica, but what upset him most was the news that his mother, Doña Maria, had died in Barcelona. When rumors of imminent war became insistent, Picasso was at Antibes with Dora Maar and Sabartès. He was worried about the works he had left in his studio and he decided to return to Paris. His friends, and above all Eluard with whom he was inseparable in those years, talked him into leaving because of the threat of bombing and going to Royan, on the Atlantic coast. Here he set himself up in a small and badly lit room, bought a supply of drawing paper, canvases, and paints and set to work as usual. He had to go to Paris to straighten out his affairs, however, and when he returned to Royan he found better lodgings in a villa called Les Voiliers.

In actual fact he was not able to stay away from the capital very long

After accepting an assignment to prepare a mural for the Spanish pavilion at the Paris World's Fair in 1937, Picasso rented two floors of a building on the Rue des Grands-Augustins for studio space. His Afghan Kazbek occupies a frame of sunlight (below, far left) and the painter (below, center) poses in front of *Guernica,* the work in progress.

The poet Paul Eluard (left, below) became Picasso's close friend during World War II and introduced him to Dora Maar (above) during a summer at Mougins. Despite fuel shortages that often left his stove without coal (right, bottom), Picasso returned to Paris for the winters. He found a warm corner to work in the lithographic shops of Ferdinand Mourlot. A flurry of lithographs such as the head of a boy (left) resulted. He also resumed sculpting (right, top) although bronze for casting was scarce.

and so he soon left Royan. Life there had started to become difficult. Little by little things became scarce—they had to do without a car, food was becoming hard to find, and there was no more heat. The winter months in the large rooms of the studio on the Rue des Grands-Augustins were now intolerable. He suffered from the cold, but refused a special offer of coal. "A Spaniard," he said, "should not feel the cold." The American consul tried to persuade him to leave France and settle in the United States but he refused.

His presence in the occupied city, despite the fact that the Nazis had termed him a degenerate artist, was a gesture of defiance. He continued to work (this was the period of the seated women), and he was often visited by German soldiers who came to ask for his autograph. Still he was not allowed to participate in exhibitions and newspapers could not cite his name. In the house he was able to heat only the bathroom and it became his studio. There he did the famous *Bull's Head* (1943), using a bicycle handlebars and seat, and painted the terrifying bull and oxhead still lifes (Plates 108, 109) and the *Reclining Nude with Musician* (*L'Aubade*), dating from 1942 (Plate 110). More than once German officers came to search his studio. One day one of them asked, indicating a reproduction of *Guernica* on the table: "Did you do this?" "No," Picasso replied, "you did."

On August 25, 1944, Paris was liberated and the painter could see his city again without anxiety, the city to which he then dedicated a series of lithographs. Immediately after the liberation of Paris he joined the Communist party, and *L'Humanité* published a photograph of him that occupied almost the entire first page. He made many statements about that decision, including the following: "My joining the Communist party is the logical consequence of my whole life. I am very pleased to say, in fact, that I have never considered painting simply as an art form for pleasure or diversion. What I wanted was design and color to be my weapons to penetrate further and further into man's consciousness, so that this knowledge can lead us a little further each day on the road of freedom. . . ."

A Volcano in Continuous Eruption

In August, 1945, Picasso was able to leave Paris and return to the Côte d'Azur, to Golfe Juan. He bought a small Provençal house at Menerbes after seeing it in a photograph. He went to see it with Dora Maar and gave it to her as a present. In the autumn of the same year Pablo was invited by the printer Fernand Mourlot to resume making lithographs. Among the first

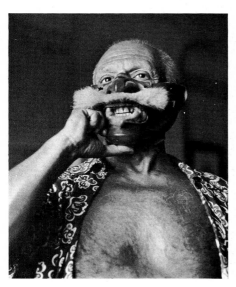

A group of friends pose with Picasso in April, 1944 (top left): Catalan painter Ortiz de Zarate, Françoise Gilot, sculptor Apelles Fenosa, actor Jean Marais, Pierre Reverdy, Jean Cocteau, and Brassaï, who snapped the picture. In 1946 Picasso moved to the Côte d'Azur with Françoise (above), where he spent some of the happiest years of his life. A son Claude (top right) was born in 1947 and then a daughter, Paloma; the new family brought out the father's clowning instincts (bottom right). The ceramic furnaces at nearby Vallauris (left, below) attracted Picasso to potting; he examines some of the results (left, center) as they come out of the kiln.

that he did was a portrait of a young girl with regular features and classical proportions. The model was Françoise Gilot and she interested Picasso because of her passion for painting and her obvious talent. From that moment on, everything that he did became a homage to Françoise, and in 1946 he moved with her to the Côte d'Azur, remaining there for a year, then to Vallauris. The new relationship with Françoise, with whom he had two children—Claude in 1947 and Paloma in 1949—lasted until 1953 and was often quite stormy. It was Françoise who left him, taking her two children with her.

When she left, the seventy-two-year-old painter, in his house at Vallauris, began to draw frantically. In nine weeks he finished a series of 180 tragicomic scenes of nude women with the old painter, with fauns, cupids, and young girls. He drew them with blind eyes, "like the goldfinches, to make them sing better." The first years that he had spent with Françoise, however, were inspired with a joie de vivre—he worked in fresco, painting a number of mother-and-child scenes, and also on lithographs and sculpture. In 1947 he discovered the ceramic works of Vallauris and, immediately falling in love with the medium, he became a potter. Vallauris became world famous. He worked

45

the clay without stopping, in his obsessive way, and in a year produced more than six hundred pieces. "He was a volcano in continuous eruption," wrote Sabartès; "his activity was a form of madness."

At Vallauris was a bullring and Picasso returned to the passion of his childhood. He became president of the jury of the fights that he went to see with his children and friends. Françoise was replaced by Jacqueline Roque, his last mistress who entered the painter's life in 1954. They were married in 1961, and she spent his last years with him and was by his side when he died. In 1955 Pablo left Vallauris and bought a large villa above Cannes, "La Californie," a nightmarish building with a large park. He transformed the old salons into a chaotic, disordered, and cheerful studio, indifferent to the varnish and gilding. There he painted and sculptured surrounded by the friends and animals, monkeys, cats, dogs, and goats that he loved.

The only thing he wanted was to work and Jacqueline succeeded in keeping visitors at bay so that he could be left in peace. Although he was by then a very rich man, Picasso never abandoned his simple habits, his careless manner of dress, and his frugality. In 1955 he collaborated in a film, *The Mystery of Picasso*, directed by Georges-Henri Clouzot, which attempted to record Picasso's creative process.

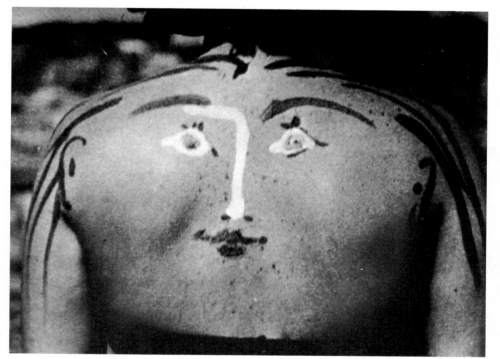

Photographs brought out the ham in Picasso: in studio on the Côte d'Azur (far left), with hands of bread at Vallauris (left), in front of panel he painted in 1958 for the Paris headquarters of UNESCO (left, above), and in frames from Clouzot's movie (right). Françoise holds an engraving of the baby Claude (top); the 1952 engraving (above) is of Paloma with a doll.

Picasso talks with Clouzot (above) whose film (frames, top left) followed the progress of drawings and paintings from start to finish. At age eighty, Picasso married Jacqueline Roque (top and in background above). They moved to a thirty-five-room villa, Notre-Dame-de-Vie, that afforded them privacy, plenty of room to store Picasso's private collection, and several studios (top right), including one big enough for works that dwarfed the artist (left).

Death of a Toreador

The human adventure of Picasso at his retreat on the Côte d'Azur does not offer many more facts for the chronicler. His artistic adventure, on the other hand, went on inexorably. Major retrospective exhibitions followed one after another all around the world from Paris to Tokyo, Milan, Rome, São Paulo, Munich, New York, and Hamburg. The world had become his fatherland because it understood his art.

For years he had been studied, criticized, and discussed. Finally he was loved without need of explanation. "Everyone wants to understand art," he once said, "but why do people not seek to understand the singing of birds? Why do they love the night and flowers and everything that surrounds us without trying to understand them? And yet, when they confront a painting they think that it is necessary to understand it. They should rather understand, once and for all, that an artist creates because he must create and he is an insignificant part of the world. We need not make more of him than anything else in the world that pleases us, even if we don't succeed in explaining him."

The last event in the story of the man Picasso is the story of his death. For the last few years of his life, he had left the villa near Cannes, because it was too open to the curious, and had bought a large country house, Notre-Dame-de-Vie, in the outskirts of Mougins. His death came as a surprise because, although Picasso was ninety-one, he had become an essential and almost inalienable part of the world. This grand old man seemed to keep death at a distance and on guard, as the toreador keeps the bull away with the point of his sword; he seemed to most people to have become immortal.

Pablo Picasso died in Mougins on Sunday, April 8, 1973, at 11:40 in the morning. For some time he had not been feeling well, but Jacqueline and his friends believed he had recovered once more. Even during that brief illness he had not stopped working. His room was full of sheets of drawing; he even worked at night, and in the morning the floor was always covered with drawings.

Picasso spent his seventh and eighth decades in the company of Jacqueline (below with portrait), a few friends (an actress from Cocteau's film *Orpheus* and her son, left, above), and his children. Paloma (above) became a painter, specializing in jewelry. Claude was introduced to bullfights on the Riviera (right and top left). Picasso had been in exile from Spain since Franco's 1939 victory in the Spanish Civil War.

Even during his illness he made sure that the large exhibition of his latest works, which was to open in Avignon at the end of May, was set up according to his directions. Paul Puaux, Director of the Avignon Art Festival, had gone to see him a few days before: "I found him exceptional as usual. One would not have dared to call him old—he didn't have the appearance of being old. With that diabolical smile of his he told me that sometimes he worked until three in the morning. I think he was enjoying the thought that he was fooling everyone who thought he was in bad health."

On Sunday, April 8, a little before midday, Picasso was still in bed in his pajamas. The wife of the gardener, Marie Barra, had brought him his breakfast and the newspapers because Emile, the cook, was having the day off. It was a rainy morning and the two Afghan dogs on the porch were barking in an annoyed way. Suddenly Jacqueline realized that Pablo was not well and ran to the bed, but the painter had already died; one hand clutched the sheet and the other was resting on a page of *Le Monde*, the newspaper he had been reading. "It must have been a painless death," reported Dr. Jean-Claude Rance, one of the family doctors. "The crisis lasted only a few seconds, and then the heart stopped beating."

By Jacqueline's orders the gates of the villa were closed to everyone—not only to the journalists who began coming to Mougins from all over Europe

but also to his painter and writer friends. Only family and a few intimate friends were allowed to the wake. The old man was laid out on his bed, smiling and dressed in grey. There were also very few at the funeral and at the burial in the grounds in front of the entrance to his Château de Vauvenargues in Aix-en-Provence. A statue from the personal collection of the artist was placed on the tomb, a work from 1934 that had not been cast until many years later. It represents the figure of a woman almost three feet high with a jug in her hand. This tomb, destined to be honored for centuries, looks out on the famous "Cézanne view" of Mont Sainte-Victoire.

A Victor

Picasso is a symbol of supreme liberty, of compulsive innovation and inevitable scandal. In popular mythology he will always be the superman of painting just as Einstein is of physics and Freud of psychoanalysis. His genius, among many qualities, had the capacity of remaining constantly at the center of discussion and passion. Without forcing his own nature, but with a sure sense of reality, Picasso was able to shape his own glory and his own popularity. "Who says that success always goes to those who try to please the public?" he said one day to his friend Brassaï. "I have shown that it is possible to be successful even going against everyone, without compromising. And at the height of my success I can do what I want—anything I want."

The writer André Malraux once said, "As long as he lives, Picasso will always be a victor." But it is more exact to say that as long as painting lives, he will remain a victor. The sculptor Jean Arp once coined the following definition: "Picasso is important just as Adam and Eve, a star, a spring, a tree, a fable, a rock, and he will always remain old and young just as Adam, a star, a rock, or a spring." He was a strong and courageous man, a great artist, and a pure genius, and he was also an extraordinary force of nature. His art is not to be explained, but to be loved. "When all is said and done," he would say, "there is nothing but love. I paint for my pain and for my joy. I place things according to my whim. I put into my painting everything that I love. Too bad for the things, they have to make do."

In the last years of his life, Picasso sought escape from the myth mania of the public, even to the extent of ignoring the celebration in honor of his ninetieth birthday. He rarely left Notre-Dame-de-Vie (below) where he died at age ninety-one on April 8, 1973.

THE PICASSO PHENOMENON

by Marco Valsecchi

Detail from *Peace*, 1952

Even for Picasso there was a period of apprenticeship, and quite a long one. Pablo Ruiz Picasso was a precocious boy. When the boy was thirteen, his father, José Ruiz Blasco, announced that he had nothing further to teach his prodigious pupil. In fact, he gave him his palette and allowed him at the age of fifteen to rent his own studio in order to freely develop his aptitudes. It must be acknowledged that the father was the first to recognize the qualities of the young painter and to encourage him even if his son's work might overshadow or even completely obscure his own name.

The boy's early precocity was further revealed when he was admitted to the Barcelona School of Fine Arts after completing the entrance-exam drawings in a single day. And the same thing happened later, in 1897, when he gained entry at sixteen to the Royal Academy of San Fernando in Madrid. But for the talent to develop fully, the apprenticeship was necessarily long. Yet it was not difficult as demonstrated by the fact that one of his first pictures, entitled *The First Communion,* was accepted for an exhibition in Barcelona and received favorable reviews.

Another youthful success occurred in 1897 when he submitted to the National Exhibition at Madrid a painting entitled *Science and Charity,* which earned an honorable mention and later, when exhibited in Málaga, a gold medal. In truth, these youthful works demonstrate a remarkable manual dexterity but also evidence of psychological immaturity normal in those years, linking naïveté with realism. It is also possible that those early successes might have been aided by the very age of the painter—they might have been the usual favors that one would concede to a child prodigy—and influenced by the knowledge that he was the son of the renowned teacher José Ruiz Blasco.

This makes it understandable that when the critics, a few years ago, were reexamining the first attempts of the famous artist-to-be, they baptized that long youthful period the time of "Picasso before Picasso." This was to emphasize that it was a period of preparation, an unripe if not utterly remote period distinct from that period of maturity that came with his many contacts in Paris, during which time the artist began to show those peculiar characteristics that distinguished him from others. In a certain sense one could say that even Picasso was conscious of that development, as revealed in the different ways in which he signed his works. At first it was Pablo Ruiz Picasso, then Pablo R. Picasso, and finally, when he gained complete independence, it became the single name Picasso. It is interesting to note that this happened in the winter of 1901 in Madrid, after his first trip to Paris in the autumn of 1900 with his friend, the painter Carlos Casagemas.

Better indications of his talent, though, are the drawings, rapid sketches, and caricatures he made in 1897 of his friends and colleagues who were frequenters of the literary cabaret in Barcelona known by the name Els Quatre Gats or the Four Cats. Picasso was then sixteen but was nevertheless treated by painters and writers as if he were a mature man. Certainly aesthetic activities in Paris could not have been excluded from the conversations at those tables. The very name of the Barcelona cabaret bore the echo of the Paris Chat Noir.

The Four Cats was where Picasso met the sculptor Manolo Hugué, the two brothers Angel and Mateo Fernandez de Soto, Joaquin Mir, Casagemas, and the tailor Francisco Soler who traded clothing for the works of a few young artists. Among the documents of that period is a very interesting drawing done in 1898 and signed P. Ruiz Picasso. It is a design for the cabaret menus whose style tending toward what was to become Art Nouveau is easy to recognize. Its broad and emphatic lines define the pattern in the manner of a group in Paris called the Nabis. The Nabis published the *Revue Blanche* which was known for its defense of Gauguin and the contributions of Symbolist poets and writers.

The Indifference of Paris

Economically, the turn of the century was an unsuccessful period for the young Picasso. But alternating between one or another friend—with Casagemas, who ended up committing suicide in a Parisian café, or with the poet Jaime Sabartés, who became his faithful secretary for almost sixty years —he managed to support himself in that rough bohemian interlude.

In the summer of 1898, he went with Manuel Pallarès to Horta de San Juan for a stay of several months. Picasso remembers that it was in that place, where he painted and drew in complete liberty, that he became what he was for the rest of his life—an independent, secure, and original painter.

On his first trip to Paris, at the end of October, 1900, he went with Casagemas to see the International Exposition, and the two young men found comfort in the hospitality of their compatriot painter, Isidro Nonell. Although they were there no longer than two months, one can say that the lights of the Ville Lumière opened up the cocoon. One can also deduce what captured Picasso's particular interest from some of the drawings of that time. In the charcoal drawing *Self-portrait*, of 1901, he is standing in his overcoat with his crumpled hat on his head. The strong influence of Toulouse-Lautrec's

Self-Portrait, 1901

thick and interwoven lines is quite evident. He is to repeat this, as a caricature of himself, in the self-portrait painted about the same time in which he is wearing a top hat with several *chanteuses* at his shoulders, just as Gauguin in his *Self-portrait* in Tahiti shows himself half nude with his palette, stretched out on the beach like a native. When he wishes to express the dances at the Moulin de la Galette (Plate 2), or the cancan, or an actress bowing on the stage, he does it similarly, more in the style of Toulouse-Lautrec than of Degas; this is clear in his forceful ability to underline an atmosphere or an unhappy face. Even his preference for pastels shows the decisive influence of Toulouse-Lautrec.

This influence prevailed during his first Paris journey and expanded even further under the impetus of experience and the curiosity of the twenty-year-old painter. Paris was in a courageous ferment of ideas and artistic reforms. Besides the works of Van Gogh and Georges Seurat, who had both died some years before, Paris offered a vast range of the type of artistic interests that can arise in a city enjoying its full political and cultural fruition. There were the influences of the Symbolists and the Nabis, Gauguin (who was in the Pacific but whose presence was felt in Paris through the *Revue Blanche*), Cézanne at Aix, Renoir at Cagnes, Monet at Giverny, the half-blind Degas at Saint-Valéry-sur-Somme or in his studio on the Boulevard Clichy, all of whom were connected with the galleries of Vollard and Durand-Ruel. Then there were the writers following the vicissitudes of the painters, from Max Jacob to André Salmon.

Poverty and various setbacks sent a humiliated Picasso back to Barcelona several times, but his thoughts had begun to center around Paris. He had to return in extreme need to his father's house in Catalonia at least four times, but each time he obstinately took the journey back to Paris. A young Catalan, Petrus Mañach, offered Picasso a possible entry into Parisian life in the form of a contract, in the summer of 1901, for 150 francs a month for his work and the possibility of an exhibition in an important gallery.

The exhibition was held between June and July in Vollard's gallery, with an introduction by the writer Gustave Coquiot. It attracted the attention of the critic Félicien Fagus who immediately recognized certain fundamental traits in the young painter: "Picasso is a painter, absolutely and decidedly a painter. His feeling for substance would be enough to demonstrate that. Like all true painters, he loves color for itself, and every substance has its color. . . . It is not difficult to discern the many possible influences: Delacroix, Manet, Monet, Van Gogh, Pissarro, Toulouse-Lautrec, Degas, Forain, and perhaps even Rops. . . . But all in passing and absorbed as soon as they are picked up. It is clear that his impetuosity has not yet allowed him to settle on any particular style. His personality is characterized by this impetuosity, by this youthful and furious spontaneity."

This critic was already aware of that rapacious capacity of Picasso's to seize upon any and all sources of cultural stimulus, even if they were contradictory, and of his ability to bend them to his own talent, successfully creating something original after sucking out all their juices, in a crescendo of

Picasso in a Top Hat, 1901

57

Women at the Fountain, 1921

inventive power. It is a trait found throughout his entire career. Independent from any academic influence, he was able to extract a new creative impulse from any epoch or culture, and it must be emphasized it was creation and not imitation. The starting point might have been a Greek vase, a piece of Catalan sculpture, an African mask, or the inspiration of Gustave Courbet, Nicolas Poussin, Delacroix, or Velásquez. But for the artist to be able to absorb them into his imagination, he must consider them as virgin material to be worked on in the same way that he might absorb the vision of a landscape. The infusion which then takes place in his mind allows him to represent them as completely new after having been lacerated, torn apart, turned upside down, and finally smoothly recomposed according to an order that depends on his own personal creative talent alone.

The favorable reception by the critic, however, did not change Picasso's personal circumstances. He had met Max Jacob, he had met André Salmon, and Sabartés had joined him in Paris. But he was exhausted and disillusioned by poverty and the indifference of the public, so he returned to his family in Barcelona and once again became a regular visitor to the literary cafés along the Ramblas.

The Blue Period

During the spring of 1902, the determination of his fellow countryman Mañach made it possible for Picasso to exhibit other works at the gallery of

Woman Ironing, 1904

58

Study for *La Vie*, 1903

Berthe Weill in Paris, one of the most avant-garde galleries of the time, along with works by other painters, including Matisse. This was an unusual event, even if the two painters did not yet know each other, because it showed that Mañach and the gallery had an awareness and an intuitive feeling for originality.

For some months the example given by Toulouse-Lautrec's depiction of the Paris *demimonde*, with the misery of the human condition his subjects reflected, had become a depressing preoccupation for Picasso. His preoccupation was not so much reflection on the unfortunate creatures themselves, but rather penetrating discernment, a way of participating in the lives of the disinherited. Paris might have offered Picasso the gilded world of the *belle époque* if he had wished. Instead he chose those strata in which pain and resignation are evident. This was his Blue Period in which he expressed with that color a sense of sadness in the world of prostitutes, old Jews, emaciated boys, and beggars (Plates 5, 6, 7, 11, 12). Such a pictorial solution was radically symbolist, even if it did not react in the same manner as a novelist like Joris Karl Huysman who depicted refined but decadent surroundings or precious and bourgeois interiors. Picasso's blues attracted the attention and favor of Charles Morice who wrote the following perceptive review in the important journal *Mercure de France:* "The sadness which permeates the entire prolific production of this young man is quite extraordinary. Picasso, who began to paint even before he had learned to read, seems to have received the mission to express with his brush everything that exists, as if told by a young god who wishes to reconstruct the world. But a gloomy god at that—the hundreds of faces he has painted are grim, without a single smile, and he shows us a world no longer inhabitable because its structures are contaminated with leprosy. His painting itself is diseased. . . . But should we hope that such painting should get well? Or is not perhaps this boy, who is so disconcertingly precocious, destined to consecrate his masterpieces to the negative side of life, the evil by which he, like everyone else, also suffers?"

Certain paintings confirm Morice's intuition: the extensive series of the *Poor on the River Bank, The Embrace* (Plate 13), recalling Maillol sculpture in its flourishing nudes; the *Old Jew* (Plate 11); the *Old Guitarist* (Plate 12); and the extraordinary portrait of *Celestina,* who is one-eyed with a cataract that whitens her pupil. All those were completed between 1901 and 1904.

Chez le Bateau Lavoir

In April of 1904 Picasso went to Paris again with money he managed to scrape together in Barcelona. This time he stayed in a wooden tenement house that had been built near the end of the Rue Ravignan, along the slope of the hill of Montmartre. It became a kind of small commune where Paco Durio, Kees van Dongen, Pierre MacOrlan, André Salmon, Max Jacob, and several people in transit lived in tiny rooms, engaged in a promiscuous mixture of work and daily existence. Max Jacob christened this large dilapidated structure the Bateau Lavoir and among the people who came and went was the woman who became Picasso's mistress, Fernande Olivier.

59

It was to this same tenement house that in 1905 Max Jacob brought Leo and Gertrude Stein, the wealthy American brother and sister who were deeply interested in art. By then Picasso had discovered the world of actors, circus performers, acrobats, and young women with monkeys. The Steins asked for a portrait and bought some pictures for a ridiculously small sum. Once again it was Charles Morice who noted the new step forward in Picasso's outlook, psychology, and style: "He no longer takes delight within himself in what is sad and what is ugly. Logically, his premature twilight of morbid depression should have led to a night of desperation and death, but by a happy inconsistency he chanced·upon a ray of light, and it brought a dawn of compassion and salvation instead."

His new psychological state also brought a development in his drawing. The heavy forms and contours gave way to a slim and delicate line and the impetus of happiness guided his touch. This change did not escape the poet Guillaume Apollinaire, who from that moment on became a faithful and intelligent ally in all the controversy surrounding the young painter. The art of Picasso excited and at the same time bothered the more perceptive of the French intelligentsia. In May, 1905, Apollinaire wrote a long essay in which he said, among other things: "Picasso's propensity for swift lines penetrates and transforms things, producing almost unique effects of linear chalcography, in which the general appearance of the world is not at all affected by lights, which modifies form by an alteration of color."

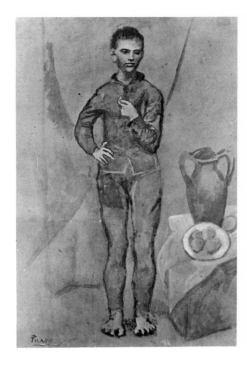

Juggler with Still Life, 1905

The Rose Period

But the change in color, which initiated the period between 1905 and 1906 and because of the predominance of light and rose colors is known as the Rose Period, was more than a psychological change. It also corresponded to an advance in quality and to a complex ripening of daily and cultural events that were closely interwoven and capable of enclosing the art of Picasso in a kind of complacent elegance, unless he kept alert his insight into form and his lucid awareness of a rigorous, unfulfilled, and continuing evolution.

Cesare Brandi contributed to a clearer understanding of this by some lines written in 1947: "As before, but in a less epidemic and better prepared fusion, the different veins flow together: Seurat, in his almost unpleasant definition of form and even in his choice of female nudes, which are, without ideal reserve, merely pleasant women of the time with their busts slightly misshapen; Puvis de Chavannes, in a certain refinement of contours and more importantly in the clear, opaque, and abstract color; likewise Degas, but surprised in an initial moment of compromise between an Ingres seen again by Puvis and the warm sensuality of a Courbet; and finally Cézanne, only touched on lightly till now but revealed in the more lively and atmospheric treatment of outline. . . . Thus are born the tender and dreamy Harlequin family, the acrobats resting on a sheath of silk, and the boys taking the horse to bathe. Here the youngsters, clothed only in their sexless softness, take their cue from Degas and renew that inexplicable kinship with horses that in some respects derives from the Panathenaea. This first hint of Classical art was so discreet that it passed by almost unnoticed (not however by Apollinaire), but it was there in the deliberate, flexible unity and in the fusion of beauty and form which is so difficult to achieve."

Brandi cites Cézanne as a hardly perceptible influence. His influence was nevertheless to appear again as soon as Picasso felt the need to harden those delicate rose transparencies. For that same reason he retired to Gosol, high up in the Pyrenees toward Andorra, in 1906 and, using Fernande as a model, painted a series of female nudes with ample thighs and well-rounded forms (such as Plate 24) recalling Catalan sculptures of the Romanesque period. He returned to Paris in the summer to escape a typhoid epidemic that had broken out in that little mountain region, and the importance of Cézanne, whose works were beginning to be exhibited, became almost inevitable. The example of the master from Aix corresponded to Picasso's own transition from an instinctive phase to intellectual meditation. We are best made aware of this in the famous *Portrait of Gertrude Stein*, 1906 (Plate 26), which displays an overwhelming sense of volume within the curved space of the armchair which acquires power with its full burden.

Already in his Symbolist Blue and Rose periods, Picasso had grappled with the crisis of realism arising from the closing of the golden age of French Impressionism. Having passed through the imitative phase, he was now playing with all the possibilities of invention beyond physical actuality rather than with interpretation. This is the reason why, when he had finished the portrait, he erased the face and repainted it, accentuating the qualities of an ivory mask. The same process took place a few days later when he did his *Self-portrait* (Plate 25), which suggests an African mask with its squared-off simplification and its geometric emphasis.

These were the first indications of Negro sculpture, which was adopted not so much for its exotic connotations but rather as a suggestion of formal autonomy from a naturalistic vision. One could even argue that Negro sculpture, which was so strongly evident in the creation of *Les Demoiselles d'Avignon* (Plate 30), convinced him of the justness of Cézanne's requirement to "treat nature with the figures of a cone, a cylinder, and a sphere." But between Cézanne, who belonged to the Impressionist generation, and Picasso, who belonged to the avant-garde generation of the new century, was a chronological separation of forty years. Their respective ideals, therefore, could not possibly be the same. In this crisis—the crisis of visual transcription—Cézanne could not forget his background and long career as a naturalist painter. Even when he used geometric solids to make his works impressionistic, his transmutation of light gave a too fragile and too instantaneous effect. There was something permanent, some imprint of Classicism that Cézanne took from Poussin that always made his idealism result in an image of nature. Picasso went beyond this naturalistic basis. He used thoughts and things that were suitable for creating an image, not for imitating it from nature. Thus he was able to create a reality that stood independently, on its own, and for which nature was only a point of departure, if not quite a mere support. This was a conclusion that was reached by those same Impressionists after 1880. When

Monet, with his series on Rouen Cathedral painted at different times of the day, achieved the culmination of his luminous effect, then, in fact, he had also shown that the positive foundation of the immutability of nature, transmitted by Courbet and the Realists, had been ousted by his light effects. They seemed to change not only the momentary appearance, but even the very substance and materials of his reality.

In the paintings between 1907 and 1909, that is between the *Demoiselles* and the landscapes of Horta de San Juan, Negro art enters at first with disturbing, even savage violence, displacing any preceding sweetness that was either too sad or had a too cultivated, precious air. If there is a paroxysm contained in the *Self-portrait* in the Prague Museum or in the *Still life with Skull*, it is a paroxysm of rigorously constructive form. In fact, Picasso became aware immediately that such a rigor would be much more forceful if he played down the chromatic tones and used the colors of bark mixed with gentle shades of ash grey and amber, with the color of toasted bread, and with delicate, humid greens.

Cubism

Picasso challenged the vestiges of Naturalism in yet another way, by upsetting perspective. The whole image was either projected onto the primary plane or vertically diminished, like a superimposition of cubes. This is precisely what constitutes Cubism, according to a definition that seems to have come from Matisse, the creator in 1905 of rhythmic arabesques in his painting *La Joie de Vivre*, which is at the extreme opposite of what Picasso was trying to do. To Matisse, with all the burden of the brightness of his intelligence and mental elegance, color was an emotive invention; to Picasso, on the other hand, color was an attribute of his mental reconstruction of space.

Cubism is linked with Picasso and Braque to such a degree that a false problem arises: Who was the initiator of Cubism? The problem is false because the difference between the two artists in thought, temperament, and method is quite evident: one was a Spaniard, dramatic and restless, aggressively disquieting; the other was lucid and rational, with a deductive French intelligence and a calm and reflective way of going about things.

Given these different intellectual and psychological characteristics, it was inevitable that their respective works would be born from different motivations. Picasso's seemingly arrogant statement, "I don't search, I find," is rather a radical affirmation of his whirling intuition, which was greedily searching for new expressions through the unrestrainable forcefulness of his imagination. He was intolerant of theories since he was absorbed in the supreme pleasure of seizing upon the image, as if it arose from a sudden and agitated blooming, after he had soaked up with an avid curiosity all possible pictorial experiences accumulated from past and recent tradition.

Head of a Woman, bronze, 1909

Braque's statement, "I love the rules that correct emotion," demonstrates the counterpoint to instinct in his preference for a method of reflection proceeding from intellectual deduction, with a sense of internal measure and discipline that allows him to produce new images with tenacious wisdom. It

62

Silenus and Companions Dancing, 1933

was Apollinaire who introduced Braque to Picasso in 1907. The cards were already on the table for both of them because of their common derivation from Cézanne. Both were to play a game that was the equivalent of modifying not only this or that rule of painting but of changing the way of looking at the world.

Braque, as a Frenchman, developed a way of painting that was more cautious in its chromatic tones and more shrewdly distilled; Picasso, as a Spaniard, investigated and brought out certain rather calculated relationships. In either case, one must keep in mind what Picasso said about the formation of Cubism, with reference to the fundamental nature of the situation rather than with irony: "When we made Cubism, we had no intention of making Cubism, but only wished to express what was within ourselves."

Once this justification of the structural content of a painting was established, all the successive stages of Cubism were corollaries that clarified and asserted themselves at the same time. The first period, until 1909, can be defined as "Cézannian" because of Picasso's obstinate reconstructing of the volume of a given object or figure. The figures dating from 1909—women seated, women with their hands crossed, portraits of Vollard and other friends,

Still Life: *The Table*, 1928, Georges Braque

a woman with a mandolin, still lifes of bottles and guitars (Plates 36-42)—introduced the inverse operation of reducing the components of volume onto a plane, like an intellectual vivisection. The idea was to arrange the forms in a plane so that an object or figure could be recognized not through perspective illusion, but through an analysis of its form, and also so that it could be seen from several points of view. These multiple analyses of a total vision were put into a single image, thus giving an immediate unity to what has been seen, deduced, and imagined. At this point it was Braque who said: "One must not imitate what one wants to create."

If Cubism had stopped at the stage of exalting Cézannian structures, it would have stopped right on the threshold of the process of breaking with the Renaissance tradition. The fundamental turning point in the invention of a

Fan, Salt Box, Melon, 1909

Bust of a Woman, 1909

new sense of space and of a new concept of pictorial representation was born with Analytical Cubism and from the desire to bring together all the multiple aspects of an object and to reduce them to the plane of the painting, like a summation all at the same time of all the different instances of poetic and rational perception. The purpose was no longer to imitate, but to achieve a pictorial reality that was an absolute creation in itself.

Analytical Cubism begins with the real thing but, by omitting the empirical or scientific pretense of illusionistic perspective, achieves a reconstituted reality by purely pictorial means. One should understand that in their search for a proof of such autonomy Picasso and Braque felt the necessity of eliminating bright colors and of intoning their paintings with low notes, almost like a countermelody, so as not to disturb the formal clarity of their dissections.

Cubist Synthesis

In following this type of analysis, however, the two artists reached a point where they experienced profound dissatisfaction. The vivisection of form and the reduction onto a single plane created the difficulty of how to read the painting. Even if the title offered a clue and even if the work was to be enjoyed for its purely pictorial reality and not for its subject, a kind of obscurity still resulted that made it difficult to recognize the object or the figure. Tied as he always was to the real world, Picasso realized the danger of losing contact with daily existence. Although in his contact with life he acted with the maximum amount of freedom, he was still extracting his creative impulses from it. Cubism cannot be considered a step along the path to abstract art. The latter was derived from other situations that were thought to be totally detached from the natural world. Cubism, on the other hand, had its constants in the world of nature. If the procedure of analysis of form initiated by Cubism led to abstraction, then abstraction should be considered a derivation.

Thus there arose from this dilemma the necessity of reestablishing a synthesis with reality. Not a description, not an analysis so violent that it leads to the dispersion of the natural object, but a synthesis of time and space and of the various moments of seeing and of knowing.

During these same months, other avant-garde artistic ideas were being proposed in various parts of Europe. Futurism had moved from Paris, where Filippo Marinetti had published its first manifesto in *Le Figaro* in 1909, to Milan for painting and Florence for literature. In Munich the *Blaue Reiter*, a group of artists with revolutionary aims, was beginning to be active under the leadership of Kandinsky, Franz Marc, and Paul Klee, and later Robert Delaunay. In Russia, after the abstract Rayonism of Mikhail Larionov and Natalya Gontcharova, which derived from some of the ideas of Futurism, the Suprematist movement arose with the works of Casimir Malevich, in which the pursuit of ideal absolutism evoked geometric figuration. In Turin the Italian Chirico was discovering the interrelating enigmas between reality and irrational phantasy. Duchamp introduced the first ideas of Dadaism in his *Nude Descending a Staircase*; in New York the first inklings of Dadaist mockery began to appear from the group exhibiting at the Stieglitz gallery. Art, then, was beginning to reflect the radical overthrow of Naturalism in the subjectivity of Symbolism, which had been launched in the late 1880s.

The Collage Is Born

Picasso first tried a contact with reality by introducing alphabetic letters and numbers in the painted image (Plates 44–49), at first as pure compositional elements but soon after as indications of suggestions of reality, whether they appeared as a newspaper headline, or in small independent phrases such as *"Ma Jolie,"* which ambiguously could apply to the pleasure of painting the picture, to the countryside at Céret in the Pyrenees, or to his mistress.

Subsequent to the letters of the alphabet, he began to insert actual objects in the painting—heterogeneous materials, paper, sand, chalk—true and proper fragments of objective reality (Plates 51-53). These served as alternatives to the actual paint, and at the same time they accented the strictly pictorial and decorative value, as well as giving contrast and relief to the traditional plain surface of the painting, playing with the real object within the scheme invented by the imagination. Thus, in 1912, collage was born; it was to become a consuming passion of the art world. It was not a matter of imitating reality, but of incorporating the random object into the picture, at first in the metaphoric sense but then gradually in a literal sense, taking care, however, not to place the object according to a realistic illusion but with imaginative freedom.

Nude Figure, not dated

Using different materials and types of paper imitating wood and flowers, Picasso started to use bright colors once again because they offered a new way of increasing the distortion of the object from its context in physical reality toward a more poetic context. Once the necessity for perspective has been dispensed with, the objects and the figures immediately assume an essential compositional role in the painting. Atmosphere and light are no longer meteorological phenomena, but are used as purely creative phenomena. On this anomalous assemblage of objects, which are now newly identifiable but suspended from their literal meaning, there descends a uniform light, without any shadows to bring a return to realistic illusion. This method of breaking up areas of color with accents heightens the decorative, arabesque-like element.

This period of Cubism was extremely important in its affirmation of antinaturalist principles. Roger Fry wrote a perceptive description of it: "Synthetic Cubism, with which Picasso was involved until 1921 in a continuous variety of applications, is, in conclusion, the conceptual notation of forms equivalent to objects in the visible world, without being in any way an illusionistic representation of those objects." This direction was taken by the art of our century with a kind of drunken, creative blissfulness, as if human intelligence had cast off its reins. For almost sixty years, Picasso was the most coherent and reckless protagonist of this movement, offering to contemporary man a sense of infinite freedom of mind and imagination.

Painting up to that time had been a "plain surface with colors placed on it in a certain order," according to Maurice Denis. But with collages made up of different materials, painting acquired the effect of bas-relief, blurring the borderline between painting and sculpture, which had always been held impassable. In a certain sense, Cubism opened up an immense range of intellectual and imaginative freedom, and it was due to this sense of creative newness offered to the artist that it became so widely accepted. Other sculptors such as Lipchitz, Alexander Archipenko, and Henri Laurens took their direction from some examples of Picassian sculpture, and other painters such as Fernand Léger and Juan Gris were also influenced. A group called the *Section d'Or* (Jacques Villon, Albert Gleizes, Jean Metzinger, and others) tried to systematize the empirical principles of Cubism with mathematics and scientific deduction, but they did not rigorously apply them, as they wanted to keep their freedom. Then in 1916 the Zurich Dadaists sought to amplify the possibilities of collage to include protest and mockery, using the real object as a shocking destruction of all rational limits.

Various Polemics

Not everyone, however, applauded Cubism. Apollinaire had joined ranks with Picasso and Braque, and because he published a reproduction of a piece of sculpture by Picasso in the *Soirées de Paris*, he lost his position as editor. In 1912 the Futurists came to Paris for their exhibition at Bernheim Jeune's and began a controversy with the Cubists, maintaining that Cubism was too static and that as a result of machines and greater speed, modern life was better represented in the principles of plastic dynamism, of interpenetration of bodies, and of simultaneity of conditions of the spirit. Abstract artists refused to consider the real object at all, whereas the Cubists had kept it as a fundamental part. These polemics and disputes, in favor and against, succeeded in putting artistic theory in ferment all over the world. It all confirmed the prophecy of Picasso's friend, Eugène d'Ors, who had foreseen that this complete departure from the past would stir up a hornet's nest.

When the war broke out, many artists were dispersed. Braque was drafted and his association with Picasso was interrupted. According to Gertrude Stein, many of Picasso's collages were destroyed or scattered in his move from Paris to Montrouge. In any case it was quite evident that by 1915, a new Cubist phase had begun. This was more meditative and severe, with more emphasis on the essential purity of form and mineral colors. The geometry took on a simpler rhythm, and the drawing, done in clear, clean strokes, seemed to derive from a Raphaelesque concept of mental and harmonic order. Critics have called this phase of Picasso's Cubism the Crystal Period.

The Crystal Period

Geometric squaring of contours and a glassy clarity of color became a prevailing characteristic of this period. The geometry emphasized planes in square and rectangular rhythms and the sharp line. The geometric spaces are filled with flat, bright colors with clearly defined edges. The costumes of Harlequin and Pulcinella allow for great variety in their colored squares. The most representative work of this phase is the 1915 *Harlequin*, which leads, by way of consistent development of images, to the superb creation of the *Three Musicians* (Plate 70), of which there are two versions, both from 1921. The rhythmic squaring of geometric figures, together with the effect of the sharp edges brought about by contrasts of color, gives the impression of a syncopated allegro in musical jazz.

In those years between 1916 and 1925, Picasso became involved with the theater and came under its spell. He was at that time friends with the musician Erik Satie and the writer Jean Cocteau. The latter had already met Serge Diaghilev, the Director of the Russian Ballet, and together they had put the ballet *Le Dieu Bleu* on the stage in Paris in 1912 and the following year in London. It was not a success, but they did not give up their intention of creating a new theatrical experience. Cocteau persuaded Erik Satie to write the music for a new ballet, *Parade*, and then in 1916 he persuaded Picasso to design the scenery and the costumes. In February, 1917, Picasso went to Rome with Cocteau in order to meet Diaghilev, who was working at the Costanzi Theater for the ballet season. He stayed there a month, living on the Via Margutta. At this time he also met two young Russians, the ballet dancer Léonide Massine and the musician Igor Stravinsky. He also met the ballerina Olga Koklova, whom he married in Paris in 1918.

Harlequin, 1915

The Russian Ballet

The ballet *Parade* was performed in Paris on the evening of May 18, 1917. The drop curtain was decorated with Harlequin and Pierrot figures and other circus characters, with a large white horse and a ballerina in tutu in the foreground. It was a great success with the public. Picasso had set aside his Cubist theories for this curtain.

The ballet, however, was rejected by the public, because they felt it was too abstruse and was accompanied by strange music, which seemed to consist only of "noises."

In 1918, just before marrying Olga, Picasso had an exhibition in Paris with Matisse in the new gallery of Paul Guillaume. He went for a short stay to Biarritz and then returned with enthusiasm to the theater, where he designed more scenery and costumes for Diaghilev's ballets, *The Three-cornered Hat, Pulcinella, Quadro Flamenco, L'Après-midi d'un Faune*, and *Antigone*.

In these he alternated avant-garde motifs with more classical interpretations. This theater activity put Picasso in a position in which he was working with other artists in different fields, from Cocteau to Satie and Stravinsky, as well as various dancers, giving him a continuous variety of experiences in a creative activity that demanded the resources of the imagination in a very particular way. The results of this can be traced in his paintings, which reflect a continuously animated cultural and emotional freedom.

The Crystal phase of Cubism, around 1920, began by recalling some of the theater types that had already inspired his imagination in the quiet motifs of his Rose Period, namely the Harlequins and masked figures of the *commedia dell'arte*. Then it became strongly influenced by Picasso's experience with scenography and his contact with the poetic texts of Cocteau, the intellectual music of Satie, and the rhythmic rigor of Stravinsky. Without doubt at the vertex of this phase are the two paintings of the *Three Musicians*.

An evolution had taken place from a purist idea to a monumental idea, prompted by recollections of Roman statues and paintings. The result was a set of giant drawings and paintings attuned to antique monuments: women dressed in peploses and draped tunics that bring to mind the fluting of columns; large heads with cowlike eyes; ponderous blocks of static masonry. Rather than stopping at psychological motifs, Picasso tended here to represent the presence of antiquity, with his huge monumental nudes posed around fountains and his Michelangelesque sibyls.

Mediterranean Still Lifes

For some time Picasso had enjoyed spending part of the year working in southern France. In the summer of 1919 he was at Saint-Raphael on the Mediterranean. For him it was a period of particular well-being, both physical and intellectual, and this is reflected in his still-life paintings of objects shown before a window opened wide to a sea-blue sky (Plates 77, 78). The paintings are bathed in light and brilliant color and have cleanly cut geo-

The Sculptor and his Model, engraving, 1933

Two Drinkers, engraving, 1933

69

metric profiles that give the impression of very luminous pieces of marquetry. They still contain the stressed and syncopated rhythm derived from the *Three Musicians* but are more frenetic and at the same time more lucid because of the unexpected combinations of forms and colors. The influence of music is seen again in the presence of musical instruments in some of the still lifes from this period (Plates 79, 80). In the same way Picasso's pictorial experience acts on the imagination of his musical colleagues. For example, certain aspects of this are seen in versions of Stravinsky's style, which vary from the peasant folklore and fauve elements in *L'Histoire d'un Soldat* and *Petrouchka* to the classic quality of the Apollo myth. It was not by accident that plaster casts of Roman and Greek heads appeared in Picasso's paintings dating from around 1925, alongside musical instruments, fruits, and colored geometric marquetry patterns.

The Frenzied and the Grotesque

Picasso was to be attracted to the theater world again at other times. In 1924, the ballet *Marcuse* was put on stage by Massine, who had broken away from Diaghilev. The music was by Satie, and the scenery and costumes were designed by Picasso. It was a failure, and it failed again when it was repeated by Diaghilev in 1927. The reduction of Mount Olympus to a burlesque of jesting gods engaged in worldly pleasures, for the sake of playing with scenic effects, did not please anyone. But in it Picasso expressed a new stylistic accent. The geometric marquetry gave way to a dynamic intersection of lines. In the works immediately preceding this he had expressed his delight in static and geometric purity; but now all was movement, a violent and almost grotesquely demonic outburst. An outstanding example of this different creative spirit is found in the painting *Three Dancers* (Plate 83), done in 1925. Three figures are caught up in the frenzy of jazz, the continuous line of their profiles twisting in broad and dynamic movement, and the colors blending into this delirium of convulsive motion, stamped like blasts from a trumpet onto the painting. The composed geometric purity of Picasso's Harlequins is swamped by the barbaric invasion of these three dancing figures. The distortions of Negro masks are brought once more to the fore, with an unusual contrast created by the surroundings of a room with stylized flowers on the walls and a deep blue window, creating an immediately unreal space in sharp contrast to the frenetic movement of the figures.

Breton had just published his first *Manifesto of Surrealism*, and he and his group of writers and poets—Paul Eluard, Louis Aragon, Benjamin Péret, Philippe Soupault—took up the defense of both the ballet *Mercure* and Picasso's new paintings. They had realized immediately that there was a great deal of exciting potential in the new Picasso and especially that rational control had been ousted from the operation of painting by an unrestrainable spirit of invention, which once again displaced all conventions, even his own preceding ones, giving way completely to an emotional excitement that transcended the cultural strata of his intellect and reached back into the obscure origins of his internal tumult. Significantly, this was in 1925, exactly the

Painter and Model, 1928

70

Girl with Monkey, 1954

year that Picasso exhibited in the first Surrealist show at the Pierre Gallery in Paris and that he published some remarks in the review *La Révolution Surréaliste*. If he did not adhere to the Surrealist movement, he certainly was in sympathy with it.

Picasso as Surrealist

It is difficult to say whether or not Picasso accepted the Freudian psychoanalytical explanations for subconscious inspiration. But it is more convincng to assume that it was his own completely creative sense of freedom that overthrew all the accumulated stratifications of tradition and that it was his own powerful capacity to produce images, to vary them in a continuous evolution, and to modify the original idea that permitted him to capture, time after time, the phantasms flashing through his imagination. It was not an abandonment to the obscure flow of the unconscious, but an extraordinary control of the image that arose from that sense of complete freedom. His mind could take in the temptations of intellectual malice: the simultaneous contradiction of the front view with the profile of the face

71

in *The Dream*, 1932 (Plate 91) and the two views, side and front, projected at the same time in *Seated Woman*, 1927 (Plate 84); or the monstrous apparition of a woman with a tongs-shaped head and boneless limbs in *Seated Bather*, 1930, a veritable premonition of Dantesque punishment; or the flabby anatomical distortion of a young woman seated in front of a mirror in *The Muse*, 1937. And then suddenly all these painful phantasms could be dissipated with a sparkling still life showing a jug and a fruit dish rhythmically sectioned out in black. The resulting inlay effect sets off the flat and transparent color, giving the effect of sun shining through stained glass. But what attracts the attention most is the constant control of the image, the drive of his restless and visionary imagination toward creations of profound and expressive insight. If there is an abandonment to the emotions, there is at the same time the contrary influence of his iron-willed mind controlling every exigency. The mythology may be obscure and disquieting, but the pictorial translation is effected with a clarity that is pitiless.

Seated Bather, 1930

Imaginative Sensuality

In 1933, and again in 1934, Picasso returned to Barcelona and then to Madrid and Toledo. In a certain sense it might be said that Picasso always remained Spanish, meaning that his mind was always stimulated by certain themes that are deeply representative of the Spanish soul: melancholy, the sense of death, the orgasmic liberation of the imagination, a certain fanciful lasciviousness, the profound stratifications of diverse cultures, and an attraction for the sun and for the obscure enchantment of dramatic perception. The appeals that he makes from time to time to Goya, or Velásquez, or El Greco are not only motivated by the cultural exigencies evident in any artist. They are a return to the ancestral strata of his origins. This return is better understood in his paintings with typically Spanish subjects such as those with bullfights or bulls.

Girl Before a Mirror, 1932

These are recurrent themes exactly for this reason, and Picasso approaches them in a variety of ways, from the bright and colorful displays of his earliest bullfight scenes at the beginning of the century to those in which the encounter, the struggle, and the drama are more important than the folklore. The bullfights painted after this trip to Spain, for instance, are dominated by the bull as a mythological symbol of violence, drama, death, and rebellion. In the *Bullfight* of 1934 (Plate 93), every element in the painting contributes to this dramatic encounter: the black bull and the blue horse are wound together in a terrible simplification of lines, fierce mouths, horns, and hooves. They fill the whole arena with a majestic tangle of violence and death. One becomes aware that his bullfights go beyond the mere memory of a popular festival and represent, rather, a mythology that expresses the apprehensions, the morbid intuitions, and the protest of the man Picasso. They are a warning of the drama that was to assail the human race only a few years later.

Without any doubt the images created by Picasso were born from his pictorial imagination and are the filter and synthesis of his entire creative adventure, and we must consider them within this dimension of originality.

They do not need any other justification to ensure their presence (fatal presence I would say) in the history of contemporary art. It is sufficient to consider only his style and his creativity of forms for them to be seen as fundamental contributions to the artistic activity of our time.

I have already mentioned the profound relationship between Picasso's imagination and the real world. He was able to use it with a maximum amount of creative liberty, but he was not able to do without it. As a man, therefore, it was impossible for him to ignore the causes of happiness, restlessness, and misfortune. One could say that becoming as he did a part of history (which is always and primarily man), he was able to tell of its terrors, its threats, its tears, its joys, and its rebellions. Certainly his heads with their absurd and grotesquely spread-out profiles, which some call "monsters," are never ironic, and this is already an indication of the moral climate that pervades the artist. They rise above it all on a plane of stylistic elaboration. But they would lose their living quality if they did not also allude to that depth of human participation that is always active in Picasso's imagination. He announced the approach of the drama. Without fear of forcing the interpretation, we could say that his grotesque women, his cruel children who strangle birds, and his fierce cats are all a direct projection of the violence that takes possession of and overwhelms mankind. His images from the decade after 1930 indicate the barbaric level reached by a civilization that was blinded by the myths of wealth, exploitation, and violent power to the point of having lost any feeling not only of piety, but also of solidarity. Certain of his deformed faces and twisted anatomies go beyond the domain and become moral portraits of a society of tyrants and victims.

Picasso denounced the monstrosities of his time and, as the increasing menace and then the violence of actual war and bombings became worse and worse, he painted *Guernica*, 1937 (Foldout opposite), in which the mythology of the bull is identified with the tragedy of the Basque city that was bombed during the Spanish Civil War, foreshadowing other atrocities to come—the bombings, deportations, and gas chambers of World War II.

The Protest of Guernica

There is an eyewitness account of this bombing of Guernica by Padre Onaindia that describes the tragic encircling of airplanes at dusk on an evening in April, 1937. They flew very low and with bombs and machine guns hit the houses, the woods, and streets, which were filled with old people, women, and children. For a little while it was not possible to see more than a hundred meters because of the smoke. The entire town was on fire, cries and moans could be heard everywhere, and terrorized people were down on their knees with their arms lifted to the sky.

As an artist concerned with the dignity of man, Picasso could not remain indifferent, and in fact he never had been. Beyond depicting the tragic mask of violence that had been perpetrated and suffered, he expressed the tragedy with the crude vehemence with which he painted the animals, the everyday objects, and the no longer innocent children, almost as if the inferno had risen from the depths and corrupted everything. From all this we can understand that besides being an undeniably political commitment, although not to be drowned in publicity-serving rhetoric, it was a commitment for mankind and with mankind. He was in the event, just as he was among the victims. If his art ended in hedonism, it nevertheless began with participation and responsibility. He shows how not to fall into propaganda with the autonomy of artistic creation, because the reality of art does not coincide with the reality intended by politics.

When World War II broke out in 1939, he was in Antibes. Southern France bordering on the Mediterranean seemed to be excluded from the war and to suffer less from its horrors. Yet he preferred to return to Paris and to remain there throughout all the war years, even during the German occupation, as a direct challenge to the promoters of tragedy.

Liberty and Joy

The liberation of Paris and the end of the war seemed like a general liberation from all the hidden evils of civilization. In 1946 he spent a long time on the Côte d'Azur where he met Françoise Gilot. The sea gave him a joy for life and this was transferred, on canvas, into an exultant series of fauns and sirens, the ancient myths of Latin civilization harmonizing with nature and with the universe, now intact and at peace. He discovered animals—centaurs, fauns, even owls, fish, horses, and bulls—no longer as symbols of death but as inhabitants of the earth alongside men. One of the doves he designed in 1949 for a poster for the World Congress in Paris became the symbol of peace for the whole world.

Top: *Dove*, lithograph, 1949
Above: variation on a dove of peace

He rediscovered life in all its aspects, in the amaryllis, in palms, in tropical fruits and flowers, in babies, in women with horse-tail hats. One of his

Goat, iron, 1950

Drawing for *Guernica*, 1937

paintings entitled *La Joie de Vivre*, 1946 (Plate 118), is a vast composition of fauns, centaurs, and nymphs playing and dancing by the seashore, with a sailboat on the horizon. He also painted the tragic symbolism of *War*, 1952 (Plate 123), for the chapel at Vallauris and beside it, in a programmed arrangement like old paintings with biblical scenes, he painted the mythological sunburst of *Peace* (Plate 124), also in 1952.

The Furnaces of Vallauris

In his newly found perspective of liberation from nightmares and tragic presentiments, his creative vitality is manifested in the curiosity with which he explored ancient craft techniques. At a ceramic works in Vallauris he rediscovered and resuscitated man's oldest craft, pottery making and painting on terra-cotta. With the outburst of excitement with which he embarked on every creative adventure, he subjected all his old themes to a revaluation. He sculpted and he modeled, discovering new and unusual relationships between the most disparate objects. He used one image to create others in a metamorphic effect. He transformed everything. One expressive form followed rapidly on another in his inextinguishable eagerness to try new things. Joyful and happy in his discoveries, he was also insatiable. His vitality seemed to sweep away and reconstruct everything.

One sign of his total liberty was the incredible variety of his work, a multiplicity of the most contrasting ideas, all created with equal enthusiasm. From this variability was born his receptivity toward all the artistic movements of the century. Every "ism" became his, but at the same time he was ready to relinquish each one for other adventures. He repeated the same theme with even more impudent curiosity, passing from a Classical to a Baroque treatment and combining them in unexpected ways. It was almost like detachment or happiness carried away by its own frenetic activity. But beyond this primary and immediate aspect, he seemed to have the urgency of someone who wanted to enlarge the space in which he operated. He wanted to master new ways to project his intelligence, and yet at the same time he was aware of the limitations of the material, of his own self, and of his own fervor, which could also have a detrimental effect, being a source in itself of restlessness. In this respect, there are those who have thought of Picasso as a slave of his own genius.

At times he sought to confront the great examples of painting from Delacroix to Goya and Velásquez, with varying results, some successful, others not. But always, there was the marvel of his extraordinary audacity and his need to experiment which saved him from any risk of virtuosity. He was sincere in all his actions. His total creativity, the result of decades of work, is immense (thousands of paintings, sculptures, drawings, and prints) among which are some that have struck like lightning, a few failures, some that are great, and some that are bold and daring. Time will make the necessary selections. But in any case it should be said that even the failures are a testimony to his never-ending sense of inquiry, and therefore they are just as important as the successes.

It is understandable that having permeated almost a century he has fascinated and offended at the same time. He has left an imprint that cannot be erased, not so much because he was in the world for such a long time, but because of the unalterable nature of his proposals and statements. No one more than he has conditioned the world of images. Without him our century would have had a different artistic connotation. To remove him from our consciousness would be impossible; to remove him from the consciousness of future generations will not be easy. Indeed, as the sculptor Henry Moore has said: "Picasso has taught us above all to see the world in a new way."

Two Nude Women, lithographs, 1946

Bull, engraving, 1946

Bullfight, lithograph, 1946

PICASSO ON PICASSO

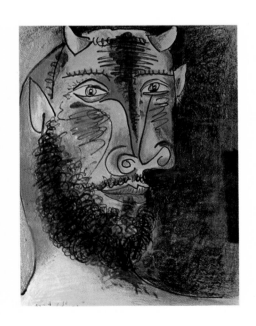

Head of a Faun, 1937

Unfortunately for me, or perhaps fortunately, I make use of things the way I want to. How sad for a painter who loves blonds not to be able to put them in a painting because they don't harmonize with a basket of fruit. How horrible for a painter who hates apples to be forced to use them all the time because they go well with the carpet. I put whatever I please in my paintings.

There was a time when paintings proceeded toward their final result in successive stages. Each day brought something new. A painting was a sum of additions. For me, a painting is a sum of destructions. First I make a painting, then I destroy it. But in the end nothing is lost, the red taken from one place turns up somewhere else.

It would be quite interesting to record photographically not the stages of a painting, but its metamorphosis. It might then be possible to reconstruct the paths the brain takes to make its dream a reality. But the most interesting thing that would be revealed is that there is no fundamental change in the painting. The initial vision remains practically intact, in spite of outward appearances. I often think of light and shade. When I put them in a painting I proceed to "break them up" by adding a color that creates an opposite effect. If the painting then is photographed, I realize that what I introduced to correct my first idea has disappeared and that essentially the image captured by the photograph corresponds to my original idea preceding all the transformations to which I subjected it.

A painting is never thought out and decided upon ahead of time, because it is subject to changes in thinking while in process, and when it is finished it continues to change, according to the feelings of whoever looks at it. A painting lives its own life just like a person. It undergoes the changes that daily life subjects it to. And this is natural, because a painting can only live through the man who looks at it.

I would like to reach a point where no one could see how one of my paintings has been made. Why? I want my paintings above all to contain emotion.

Man Carrying a Sheep, plaster, 1944

When one begins a painting one always meets with temptations. One must distrust these, destroy one's own painting, and do it over many times. Even when the artist destroys a beautiful creation, he doesn't really do away with it, but rather changes it, condenses it, makes it more essential. The completed work is the result of a series of discoveries which have been eliminated one by one. Otherwise one runs the risk of self-admiration. And for me, I do not sell anything to myself!

In reality one works with very few colors. When they are put in just the right place, the illusion is created that there are a great many.

Lithographs from *Circus* series, 1957

Abstract art never gets beyond painting. So what's the excitement? There is no such thing as abstract art. You have to start from somewhere. You can completely remove any appearance of reality but the idea of the object will somehow have left its ineradicable sign: because it is the object that has touched the artist, that has excited his ideas, that has stirred his emotions. In the final analysis, ideas and emotions are rooted in his work. They are an integral part of it even if their presence is not evident. Whether he likes it or not, man is an instrument of nature, which imposes its character and its appearance on him. In my paintings of Dinard and the ones of Pourville, I expressed practically the same vision, but you can see the difference be-

Dove and *Head*, ceramics, 1950

tween the atmosphere of those done in Brittany and those done in Normandy, and you can recognize the light of the cliffs of Dieppe. I didn't copy that light, I didn't even pay it much attention. I was simply immersed in it. My eyes saw it, and my unconscious registered its vision, and then my hands passed on my sensation. You can't go against nature. It is stronger than the strongest man! It is simpler to go along with nature. We can allow ourselves certain liberties, but only in the details.

Moreover, there is no such thing as figurative or nonfigurative art. Everything appears to us in the form of a figure. Even in metaphysics ideas are expressed through figures, so obviously it would be absurd to think of a painting without figuration. A person, or an object, or a circle are all figures, and they act on us in a more or less intensive manner. Some are closer to our own feelings, with the result that they elicit emotions that appeal to our own emotional faculties. Others appeal more directly to the intellect. It is well to accept them all. My mind needs emotions just as much as my senses. Do you think I am interested in the fact that this painting represents two people? These two people once existed but now they exist no longer. The sight of them gave me an initial emotion but slowly their real presence became blurred, and they became for me a fiction, and then they disappeared, or rather, they were transformed into general problems. For me they are not two people any more but only forms and colors, you must understand, that

Ceramic vases with heads

Woman Squatting
painted terracotta, 1953

Vase with goat's head

still express the idea of two people and that still keep the vibrations of their existence.

The artist gathers emotions from everywhere: from the sky, from the earth, from a piece of paper, from a passing form, from a spider's web. And it is exactly because of this that you can't make distinctions between things, because they're not stratified by class. You must take what you can use where you find it, but not from your own work. It would be revolting for me to copy myself, but I don't hesitate to take what I want from a portfolio of old drawings.

Scritti di Picasso (Writings by Picasso),
edited by Mario de Micheli, Feltrinelli, 1964

The academic teaching of beauty is false. We have been so deceived that we aren't even able to track down a shadow of the truth. The beauties of the Parthenon, the Venuses, the Nymphs, the Narcissuses—they're all lies. Art is not the application of a canon of beauty, but rather what the instinct and the brain can conceive of independently. When you are in love with a woman, you don't turn to a measuring instrument to learn more about her form—you love her with immeasurable desire. Yet everything has been done to try to apply a canon of laws even to love. If you look at it carefully, the Parthenon is just a house on which a roof was placed. The columns and sculptures were added because there were workmen in Athens who needed to express themselves. It is not important what the artist does, but what he is. If Cézanne had lived and thought like Jacques-Emile Blache, he would not have interested me for a single minute, even if the apple he painted had been ten times more beautiful. What interests me is Cézanne's disquietude, his genius, the torments of Van Gogh: these are the human drama. All else is a lie.

Except for a few painters who are opening up new horizons, the young people of today do not know which way to turn. Rather than going along with what we have to offer so they can react more clearly against us, they are trying hard to revive the past. And yet the world is open before us and everything needs to be made new, not repeated. Why remain so desperately tied to what has already fulfilled its promise? There are miles of paintings "in the style of," but it is difficult to find a young person who works in his own way.

I am not a pessimist and I do not detest art because I could not live without dedicating all my time to it. I love art; it is the whole purpose of my life. Everything that I do in connection with it gives me immense joy. Yet I don't understand why everyone has to be concerned with art, why they feel obliged to justify it, and why, when they talk about it, they have to reveal their own stupidity. The museums are a mass of deceptions; the majority of those who claim to be interested in art are imposters. And I don't understand why there are more prejudices about art in revolutionary countries than there are in conservative countries. The paintings in museums are full of our stupidities, our mistakes, and our spiritual poverty. We have transformed them into ignoble objects. We are tied to a collection of myths instead of feeling

83

how much personal vitality was present in the men who created them. We should have a dictator for painters—the dictatorship of a painter—to eliminate all those who have confused us, to eliminate the misrepresentations, to eliminate the results of deceit, habits, spells, tales, and a mass of other things. But good sense always comes out on top! It is a revolution against good sense that is necessary. The true dictator is always being defeated by the dictation of common sense . . . Perhaps not!

Picasso's sayings collected by Christian Zervos
in Cahiers d' Art, No. 7, December, 1935

I find it difficult to understand the importance that is given to the idea of "research" when speaking of modern painting. In my opinion, research in painting has no meaning at all. To find, that is the problem. No one is interested in following a man who spends his life with his eyes glued to the ground looking for a wallet that might have been dropped on the street. If someone finds something, it doesn't matter what, even if he had no intention of looking for it, that at least arouses our curiosity, if not our admiration.

I have been accused of committing many sins. But the falsest accusation is that I've had the spirit of research as the principal objective of my life. When I paint, my purpose is to show what I have found, not what I am looking for. In art, intentions are not sufficient, and, as we say in Spain, love must be proved with deeds and not with arguments. What counts is what one has accomplished, not what one intends to do.

We all know that art is not the truth. Art is a deception made in order to approach the truth, at least such truth as can be expressed. The artist has to find a way to convince others of the truth through his deception. If in his work he shows that he has only looked and looked again for a way to present his deceptions, then he has not accomplished a thing.

"Picasso Speaks," interview with Marius de Zayas
in The Arts, New York, May, 1923

It is the idea of "research" that has often made painting fall into abstraction. And this is perhaps the biggest mistake of modern art. The spirit of research has poisoned all those who did not understand the positive angle of modern painting, but wanted to paint the invisible and what cannot be grasped by art. Very often a picture will signify much more than the painter intended. The author is often astonished by the unexpected results. The birth of a painting is sometimes a spontaneous and unpredictable procreation. Sometimes the design proposes the object; other times the color will suggest forms that will determine the subject.

. . . We speak of naturalism, as opposed to modern art. But have you ever seen a "natural" work of art? As nature and art are two perfectly different phenomena, they cannot be subordinated to the same subject. Art gives us the possibility of expressing our conception and our understanding of what

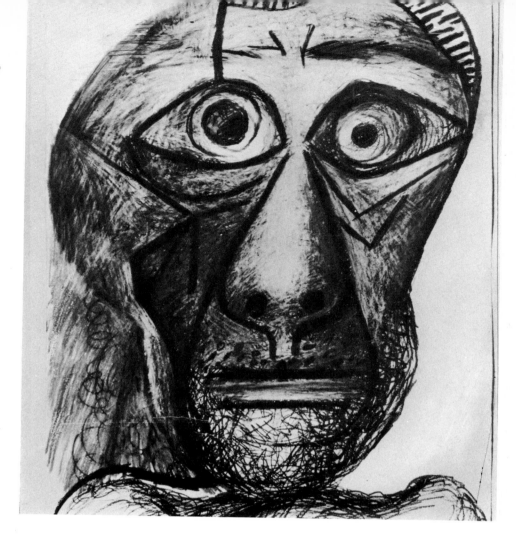

Self-Portrait, c. 1969

nature cannot give us in absolute form. Beginning with the primitives, whose art was far away from nature, up to artists like David, Ingres, and Bouguereau, who are painters of nature, it was very well understood by all that art is always art and not nature. And from the point of view of art, there are no concrete or abstract forms, but only interpretations which can be more or less conventional. These lies are necessary to guard our thoughts, as they let us create an aesthetic view of life.

Pablo Picasso to Florent Fels,
Bulletin de la Vie Artistique, June 15, 1923

I do not care about the approbation of future generations. I have dedicated my life to freedom and I want to continue being free, which means that I do not worry what will be said about me. Those who are concerned with the judgments of posterity cannot be free. Posterity is a hypothesis, and an artist does not work on hypotheses. He works for the here and now, and he works to make the here and now clear to himself and to his contemporaries.

The only one responsible for what I have done and what I do, is myself.

Art is a falsehood through which one finds the truth. Too many painters believe instead that the result of their work, that is their canvases, is the "truth" in itself. "Truth" is found beyond the canvas, never in it. It is realized in the relationship of the canvas with reality.

Nature and art are two different and distinct things, and they can never become the same thing. Some people want to express what nature "is" through art. I believe that the true function of art is to make evident everything that nature "is not."

My art is not at all abstract. Rather abstract art does not even exist and cannot exist. You can eliminate every aspect of realism and what remains is an idea which is just as real as the object which has disappeared. Art is always a representation of reality.

I look for inspiration in reality. Only reality moves my imagination and gives me new life.

I am an individualist intensely interested in everything going on around me.

I attempt to reconstruct reality.

Action and reaction, realism and abstraction alternate in my art, just as in life. My art has always been connected to life. That is reality.

Reality is only reached in silence.

In my art you can read the rhythm of the paroxysm of violence and serene meditation.

My art alternates between gracefulness and horror, comedy and violence, reflecting the two extremes of society today; there is also extended contemplation, as well as observation of the classical past.

I have painted various pictures against authoritarianism and military violence.

With my own weapons, design and color, I have wanted to conquer the conscience of mankind, so that this knowledge can lead us each day a step ahead on the road of liberty.

My greatest hope is that my work may have contributed to the prevention of future wars.

What do you think an artist is? An imbecile with nothing but eyes, if he is a painter; or ears, if a musician; or a lyre in his heart, if a poet; or a bunch of muscles, if a boxer? Of course not: an artist is also a political being, always alerted by world happenings, anguishing, passionate or pleasant as may be;

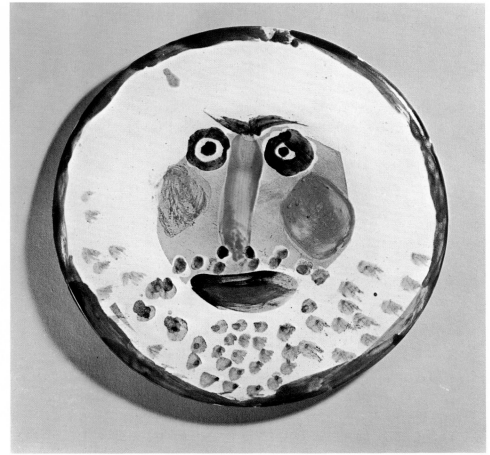

Ceramic plates: bullfighting scene, 1953, top; fighting centaurs, above; head, 1947, right; bull's head, 1957, below

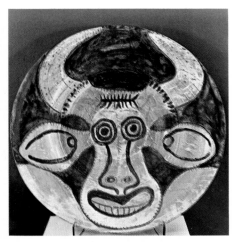

and on those happenings he shapes himself. How is it possible to be disinterested in others? And in what ivory tower of indifference could it be possible to isolate ourselves from a life that others bestow upon us with such abundance?

For me a house is an instrument for work, not a background for an elegant life. Every room is my studio, my laboratory.

I have never given up affirming my powers to invent.

Nothing interests me that does not involve a goal to reach, a problem to overcome, an enigma to resolve, or a mystery to penetrate.

My paintings depict men who are divorced from nature and civilization and are at the mercy of obscure and mysterious forces.

Mathematics, trigonometry, chemistry, psychoanalysis, music, and many other things have been cited as being components of Cubism and have been taken out of context in order to explain Cubism. But all this is pure literature, which is another way of saying pure nonsense. When we invented Cubism we didn't have any intention of inventing Cubism. We simply wanted to express what was inside us. Not one of us ever presented a project or a plan.

Cubism is no different from any other school of painting. The same principles and elements are found in every artistic experience. The fact that Cubism was not accepted for such a long time and that still today there are people who refuse it means nothing. I do not read English and because of this every English book is a blank page for me. This does not mean that the English language does not exist.

Basically I am very curious. My curiosity is greater than that of any other man. I am curious about every aspect, moment, and phenomenon of life. I am curious about every dream. My curiosity crosses over every frontier of curiosity.

Adventure is my raison d'être.

If a goal is risky, then the stimulus to reach it is stronger.

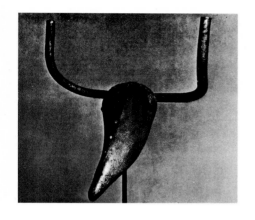

Head of a Bull, bronzed assemblage of bicycle seat and handlebars, 1943

My paintings have won a place in the panorama of contemporary art. To achieve this, though, I have had to risk something.

I work exclusively for myself, I do not seek applause, I am not interested in the opinions of others, and I don't care about what is in vogue.

In pottery, the artist can demonstrate his creativity and the forcefulness of his inventive powers just as in a painting, but with the additional advantage that he can preserve the spontaneous quality of a result that has been born concretely and materially in his own hands.

My pottery is the testimony of an old man who continues to love the world. An old man who unceasingly feels the flow of life. An old man who wants to "make" with his hands in order to be closer to the "material" of the world, the matrix of life.

Everything that I touch comes to life and becomes the incarnation of some aspect of my internal drama.

I have often tried to repeat great works of the past in my own style. I often work in several styles at the same time.

Whenever I had something to say, I said it as I felt it should be said. Different contents require a different way of expression.

It is inevitable to imitate others, it would be abject to imitate oneself.

Head and Leaf, plaster, 1943

It is not possible to copy even when trying hard. You want to copy a bull-fight, a Velásquez or a photograph: you study it well, observing it with attention, and finally you are conquered; but there will always be something that will hold back and escape. That something is you.

For me there is neither the past nor the future in art. If a work of art does not live in the present it does not live. The art of the Egyptians, the Greeks, and of the great painters of yesterday is not art of the past. It is art of today. My work reflects the commitment of a modern mind to create new and living forms.

I am a Spaniard and hence a realist, in the sense that I do not reject involvement in these two conditions of existence.

I make a dramatic contrast between light and dark for decorative unity and also because I want to emphasize the phantasmal quality of my objects.

In modern painting, each brush stroke is a precision operation; it is much like clockwork. You are painting the beard of a character. It is reddish and this color helps you to fit everything together again and to repaint all the environment, as in a sort of chain reaction. I have always wanted to avoid all this, to be able to paint as one writes, with the same swiftness of thought, following the imagination. Had I been born Chinese, I would not have become a painter, but a writer: and I would have written my paintings.

Art does not evolve by itself. The ideas of people change, and art changes in order to express these ideas. If an artist changes his way of expressing himself, it means that his way of thinking and seeing reality has changed. If the change is consistent with the changing ideas of his time then his work has improved; if not, then it has deteriorated or failed.

Whenever I have had something to say I have said it without worrying about either the past or the present.

My destiny is to work and to work without respite. I am all action and sometimes my creativity has the soul of a fury. Ideas follow one another in relation to the sensations that I am capable of feeling and the observations that I am capable of registering.

As I grow old I become less impatient.

My life has often been dramatic, never tragic.

My friends and the people I love are the direct source of my inspiration.

My landscapes are synonymous with my nudes, but people in front of my faces find that a nose is "distorted," while they are never shocked at a deformed bridge. But I make noses "distorted" on purpose because I want to force people to see, finally, a nose.

Head, bronze, 1932

An artist always works with things and emotions. Ideas? Ideas are things plus emotions. Ideas remain prisoner of the work of art. Even if the artist attempts to liberate them they cannot escape. They remain inside. They form an integral part of the work of art, even if their presence is no longer perceptible in objective form.

Solitude does not mean renunciation of the world. Rather, it means placing oneself in an observatory whence it is possible to penetrate everything in the world, but filtered and clarified, not things but ideas and emotions.

Woe to the artist who denies reality. And woe to the artist who confuses reality with the real.

Excerpts from interviews, statements, and the book
by Hélène Parmelin, *Picasso dit . . .* , Editions du Cercle d'Art et
Société Nouvelle des Editions Gonthier, Paris, 1966

FIRST
IMPRESSIONS

Furious spontaneity

Picasso is a painter, absolutely and decidedly a painter. His feeling for material suffices to prove this. Like all true painters, he loves color for itself, and to him every material has its own color.

Every subject attracts him therefore and everything becomes a subject for him: the flowers spilling forth furiously from a vase towards the light and the luminous atomsphere that dances around it; the colorful seething of a crowd, with the verdure of a race track or the hot sand of a bull ring in the background; the revelation of a female body, any female body, or its disappearance only to reappear, thickly colored, through a fluffy mass of variegated fabrics ... and there are discoveries: the clear green skirt of one of three dancing girls against the whiteness of her petticoat, made exactly with that masculine white stiffness that young girls' starched petticoats have; the white and the yellow of a woman's hat, and so on.

In the same way that any subject is an opportunity for elaboration for him, he makes everything a game in order to express it, even jargon or Gongorism (which is also jargon), and even the vernacular of the neighborhood. Nor is it difficult to detect the many probable influences in his painting: Delacroix, Manet (the most legitimate, because he also derives something from the Spanish), Monet, Van Gogh, Pissarro, Toulouse-Lautrec, Degas. . . . But they are all only passing influences, dissolved as soon as they are mastered.

It is clear that his impetuosity has not yet allowed him to settle on any particular style of his own. In fact, his personality lies in that very impetuosity, in that young and furious spontaneity (it is said he is not yet twenty, and that he covers three canvases a day). But there is also a danger here. This same impetuosity could lead him to a kind of facile virtuosity and to even more facile successes: the prolific and the fecund are two different things, just like energy and violence. It would be a shame, when he has such brilliant virility.

Félicien Fagus, "L'invasion espagnole: Picasso," in *La Revue Blanche*, Paris, July 15, 1901

A real talent

The sterile sadness that weighs down the entire prolific production of this young man is extraordinary. Picasso, who began to paint even before he had learned to read, seems to have received the mission to express everything that exists with his brush, like a young god who aims to reconstruct the world. But he is a gloomy god at that—the hundreds of faces he has painted are grim, without a single smile, and he shows us a world that is no longer inhabitable because its structures are contaminated with leprosy. His painting itself is diseased.

Incurable? I don't know, but we are certainly in the presence of a force, of a vocation, of a real talent.

Some drawings—such as a simple squatting nude—give the sensation of an absolute prodigy. Some compositions—two spectators in a theater box, a man and a woman with attention diverted from the scene where far away in full light a ballerina is twirling—attract and disturb like a *fleur du mal*; they are almost sexless beings, commonplace devils with despairing eyes, drooping heads, and foreheads furrowed with desperate or criminal thoughts.

Should we hope that painting such as this will recover? Or is it not perhaps that this boy, who is so disconcertingly precocious, is destined to consecrate his masterpieces to the negative side of life, to evil by which he, like everyone else, also suffers?

Charles Morice, "Exposition . . . ,"
in *Mercure de France*, Paris, December, 1902

A prophecy

. . . blessed are the restless in spirit, because only they shall receive eternal peace: Mir, Noñell, Xiró, and Ruiz Picasso, who with great concentration is now at work on canvases that will surprise us and even frighten us!

Eugenio d'Ors, in *El poble català*
Barcelona, December 10, 1904

Les Demoiselles d'Avignon (1907)

The problems that had kept Picasso in a turmoil of uncertainty and forced him to exploit two almost opposite tendencies at the same time found a solution in the spring of 1907. After months of work on drawings and studies, Picasso painted with determination and in the space of a few days a large picture measuring nearly eight feet square. He took unusual care in the preparation of the canvas. The smooth type of canvas that he liked to paint on would not have been strong enough for such a large surface. He therefore had a fine canvas mounted on stronger material as a reinforcement and had a stretcher made to his specified unconventional dimensions. When he still considered the picture to be unfinished, his friends were allowed to see it, and from that moment he did not work on it any more. A new style, deliberate and powerful, met their astonished gaze [Plate 30].

At first glance this picture has the power of drawing the spectator to it by its atmosphere of sheer Arcadian delight. The flesh tones of five female nudes glow against the background of a curtain, the blueness of which seems to recall the intangible depths of the sky at Gosol, but he is checked in his initial enthusiasm when he finds himself in the forbidding presence of a group of hieratic women staring at him with wide-open eyes.

Their presence is a surprise, and the small and tempting pile of fruit at their feet, poured out of a melon rind in the shape of a harlequin's hat upside down, seems irrelevant to the scene. The figure on the extreme left holds back a red ochre curtain so as to display the angular forms of her sisters. Her appearance, particularly in the grave profile of her face, is unmistakably Egyptian, whereas the two figures she reveals in the center of the picture, their tender pink flesh contrasting with the blue of the background, have more affinity to the medieval frescoes of Catalonia.

There is no movement in the three figures. Although singular and lacking in conventional grace, they are poised and serene, making a strong contrast with the two figures on the right, which, placed one above the other, complete the group. Their faces show such grotesque distortion that they appear to have intruded from another world. The figure above makes a niche for herself in the curtain, while the squatting figure below, opened out like a roast sucking pig, twists on her haunches from back to front, showing a face with staring blue eyes. Both have faces like masks which seem foreign to their naked bodies.

The opinions given by Picasso's friends were of bewildered yet categorical disapproval. No one could see any reason for this new departure. Among the surprised visitors trying to understand what had happened he could hear Leo Stein and Matisse discussing it together. The only explanation they could find amid their guffaws was that he was trying to create a fourth dimension. In reality, Matisse was angry. His immediate reaction was that the picture was an outrage, an attempt to ridicule the modern movement. He vowed he would find some means to "sink" Picasso and make him sorry for his audacious hoax. Even Georges Braque, who had recently become a friend, was no more appreciative. All he could say as his first comment was, "It is as though we are supposed to exchange our usual diet for one of tow and paraffin," and the Russian collector Shchukine exclaimed in sorrow, "What a loss to French art!"

Roland Penrose. *Picasso: His Life and Work*, New York, Harper, 1958

Figure with Vase, cement, 1933

Defense of Collage

. . . Picasso has thoroughly confronted the world. He has become used to the immeasurable light of knowledge. But at the same time he has not disdained bringing to light actual objects, a two-penny song, a postage stamp, a newspaper fragment, a piece of waxed canvas on which the fluting of a chair is painted. The art of the painting could add no graphic element to the truth of these objects.

There is savage mockery in the purity of the light in which printed numbers and letters obtrude, pictorial elements new to the art of painting although long since impregnated with humanity.

It is impossible to guess at all the possibilities or all the tendencies of an art so exacting and profound. . . .

Using planes to represent volumes, Picasso gives such a complete and incisive visual enumeration of the components that make up an object, that they become objects not through the effort of the person who looks at them and grasps their simultaneity, but purely through their intrinsic arrangement. . . .

. . . He is a newborn child rearranging the world for his own exclusive use and in order to establish relations with his equals. His delineation has epic grandeur, and with order the drama will emerge. You can argue about a system, an idea, a date, or a resemblance, but I don't see how you can argue about the simple act of delineation.

> Guillaume Apollinaire, "Picasso and the Papiers Collés,"
> in *Montjoie*, Paris, March 11, 1913

We do not agree

. . . for us [the Futurists] painting is not what I find in the Cubists, it is not the analytical enumeration of Picasso or of Braque but rather, it is life itself realized in its transformations within the object and not outside it.

We agree with Picasso in wanting to destroy painting, because we also have endeavored for several years in Italy (at first alone, but then united in Futurist solidarity) to destroy all that is old, pictorial, idiotic, traditional, realistic, decorative, discolored, and antiquated. But he is making a big mistake if he fails to realize that the search for abstract elements does not lead to an abstract construction. It is this construction which has led us to proclaim ever since the First Manifesto that the subject in art is inescapable, and it is this construction that gives a profoundly Italian character to our Futurist painting.

If then we have in Picasso an effort that tends to break away from convention (helped in this by thirty years or more of French painting) the Cubists on the contrary rush towards it. If in the former we find an abstraction that can almost be called arid, exactly like the Spanish race to which he belongs—the Spaniards have always been, in the past, the most stylized analysts—we calm and balanced Italian Futurists find in Cubism the cold refinement of French academic taste.

> Umberto Boccioni, "Futurist Painting and Sculpture
> (Plastic Dynamism)," *Poesia*, Milan, 1914

SEVENTY YEARS OF ART

1
Lovers in the Street
1900, Museum of
Modern Art, Barcelona

2
Le Moulin de la Galette, 1900
Justin K. Thannhauser Collection
The Solomon R. Guggenheim
Museum, New York

3 (LEFT)
Woman in Blue
1901, Museum of
Modern Art, Madrid

4 (RIGHT)
*The Burial of
Casagemas
(Evocation)*, 1901
Museum of Modern
Art of the City of
Paris

5 (LEFT)
The Mother, 1901
The City Art Museum
St. Louis

6 (RIGHT)
L'Apéritif, 1901
The Hermitage Museum
Leningrad

8 (ABOVE)
Pierreuse, 1901, Picasso Museum, Barcelona

7 (LEFT)
Harlequin and his Companion, 1901, The Pushkin Museum, Moscow

9
Bullfight, 1901, Stavros S. Niarchos, St. Moritz

10
The Dwarf Dancer, 1901
Picasso Museum, Barcelona

11 (LEFT)
The Old Jew, 1903, The
Pushkin Museum, Moscow

12 (RIGHT)
The Old Guitarist, 1903
Helen Birch Bartlett
Memorial Collection, The
Art Institute of Chicago

13 (LEFT)
The Embrace, 1903
Jean Walter-Paul
Guillaume Collection
Museum of the Orangerie
of the Tuileries, Paris

14 (RIGHT)
*The Acrobat's Family
with a Monkey*, 1905
Konstmuseum, Göteborg

A Sebastian Juñer
Picasso
Junio 1903

15 (LEFT)
Portrait of Sebastian Junyer, 1903
private collection

16 (RIGHT)
Woman with a Fan
1905, National
Gallery of Art
Washington, D. C.

17
The Organ-Grinder, 1906, Kunsthaus, Zurich

18
Family of Saltimbanques, 1905, Chester Dale Collection, National Gallery of Art, Washington, D.C.

19 (LEFT)
Young Acrobat on a Ball, 1905, The Pushkin Museum, Moscow

20 (ABOVE)
Seated Nude, 1905, National Museum of Modern Art, Paris

21 (LEFT)
Three Dutch Girls, 1905, National
Museum of Modern Art, Paris

22 (RIGHT)
The Two Brothers, 1906
Emanuel Hoffmann Foundation,
Oeffentliche Museum, Basel

23 (LEFT)
La Coiffure, 1906
Metropolitan Museum of Art
New York

24 (RIGHT)
La Toilette, 1906
Albright-Knox Art Gallery
Buffalo

25
Self-Portrait, 1906, A. E. Gallatin Collection, Museum of Art, Philadelphia

26
Portrait of Gertrude Stein, 1906, Metropolitan Museum of Art, New York

27 (LEFT ABOVE)
Head, 1907, private collection

28 (ABOVE)
Study for *Les Demoiselles d'Avignon*, 1907
National Museum of Modern Art, Paris

29 (LEFT)
Study for head, 1907, private collection

30 (RIGHT)
Les Demoiselles d'Avignon, 1907
Museum of Modern Art, New York

31 (LEFT)
Woman with a Fan, 1908
The Hermitage Museum
Leningrad

32 (RIGHT)
The Dryad, 1908
The Hermitage Museum
Leningrad

33 (ABOVE)
Woman with Mandolin, 1908, private collection

34 (RIGHT)
Loaves and Bowl of Fruit on a Table, 1909, Emanuel Hoffmann Foundation, Oeffentliche Museum, Basel

36
Seated Woman, 1909, private collection

35
Horta de Ebro (The Factory), 1909, The Hermitage Museum, Leningrad

38 (ABOVE)
Woman with Mandolin, 1909, The Hermitage Museum, Leningrad

37 (LEFT)
Seated Woman, 1909, Sheldon H. Solow, New York

39 (ABOVE)
Portrait of a Woman, 1909, private collection

40 (RIGHT)
Seated Woman, 1909, private collection

41 (ABOVE)
Woman in an Armchair, 1910, National Gallery, Prague

42 (RIGHT)
Portrait of Ambroise Vollard, 1909–10, The Pushkin Museum, Moscow

43 (ABOVE)
Violin, 1912, The Pushkin Museum, Moscow

44 (RIGHT)
Bottle of Pernod, 1912, The Hermitage Museum, Leningrad

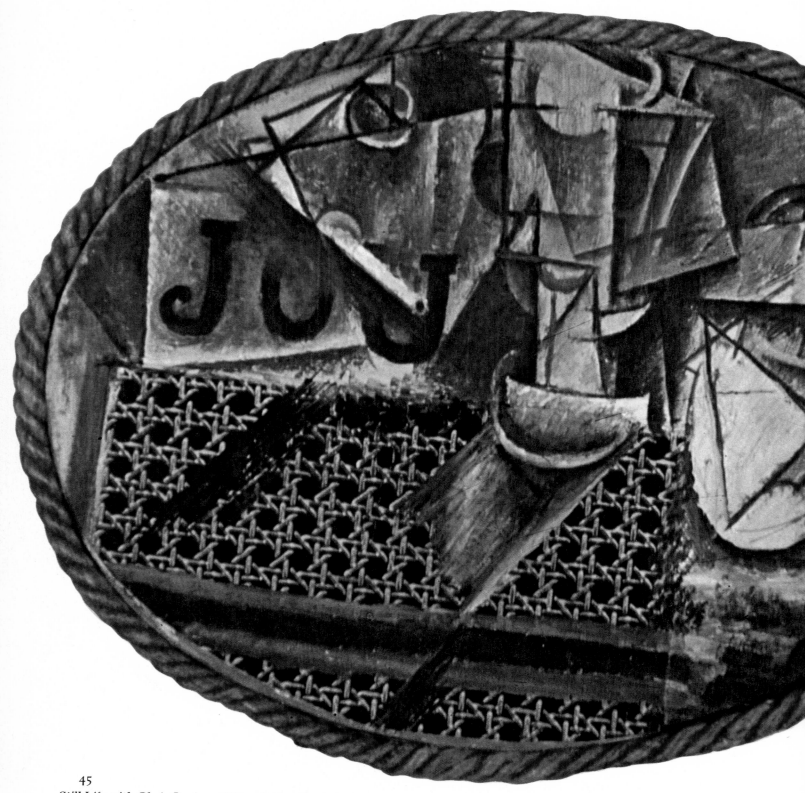

45
Still Life with Chair Caning, 1912, artist's collection

46
The Aficionado, 1912
Emanuel Hoffmann
Foundation
Oeffentliche Museum
Basel

47
Still Life "CORT," 1912, private collection

48
Pigeon with Peas, 1912, Museum of Modern Art of the City of Paris

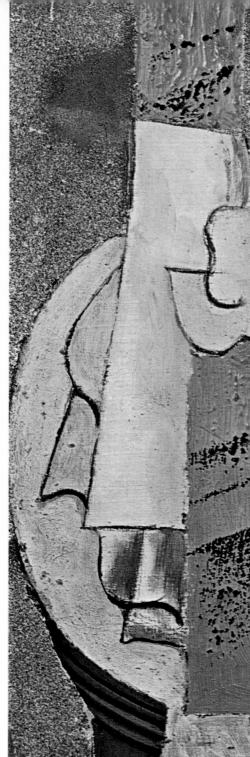

49

Vieux Marc, 1912, National Museum of Modern Art, Paris

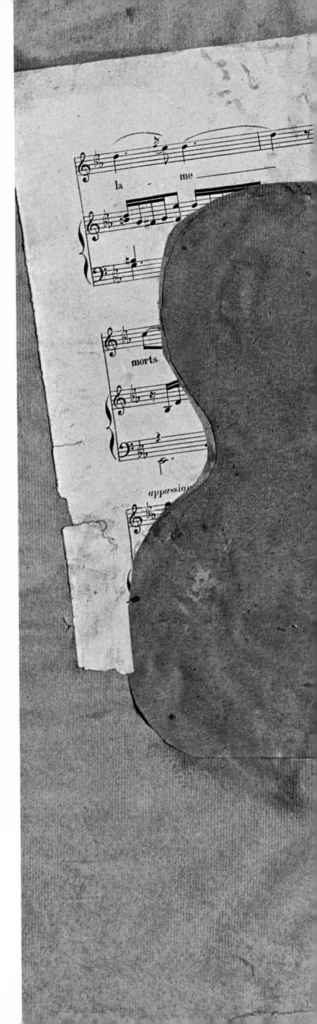

50 (ABOVE)
Violin and Clarinet, 1913, The Pushkin Museum, Moscow

51 (RIGHT)
Sheet of Music and Guitar, 1913, National Museum of Modern Art, Paris

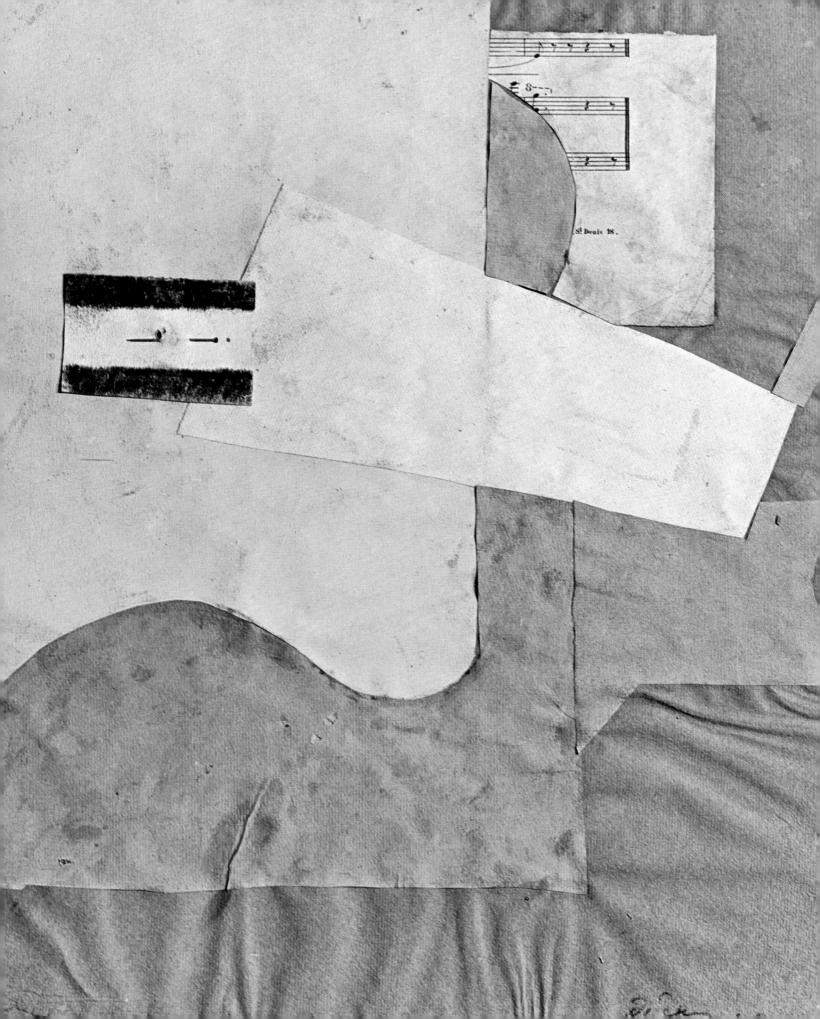

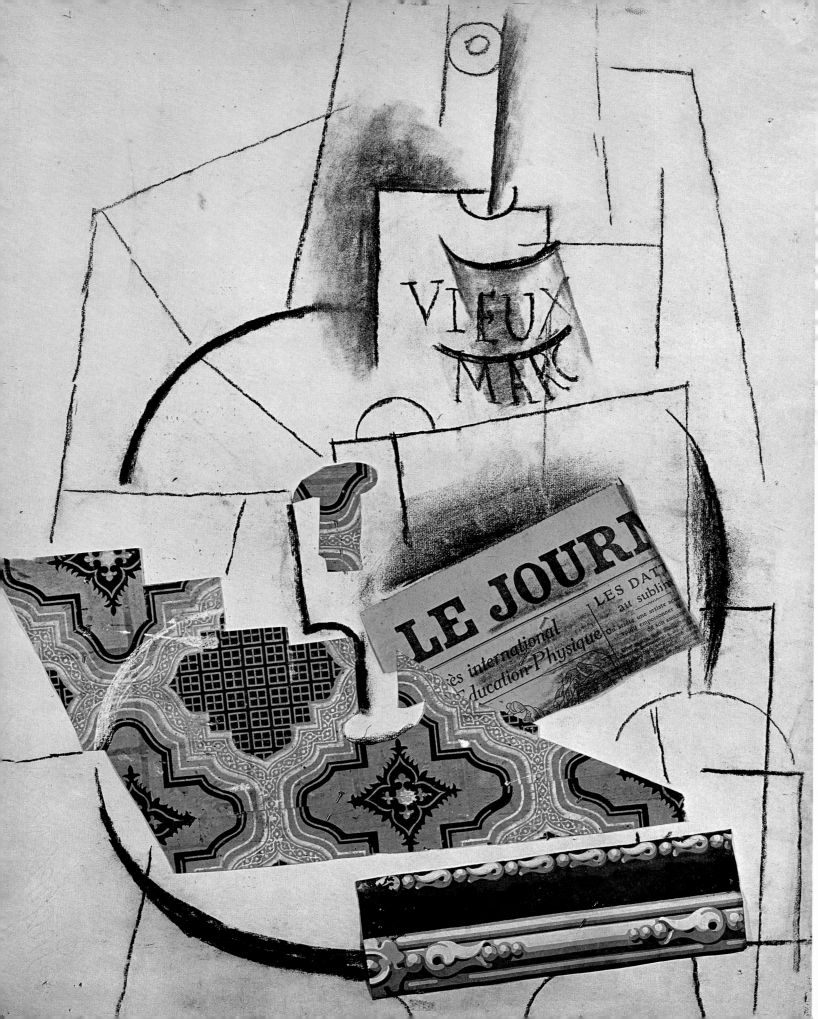

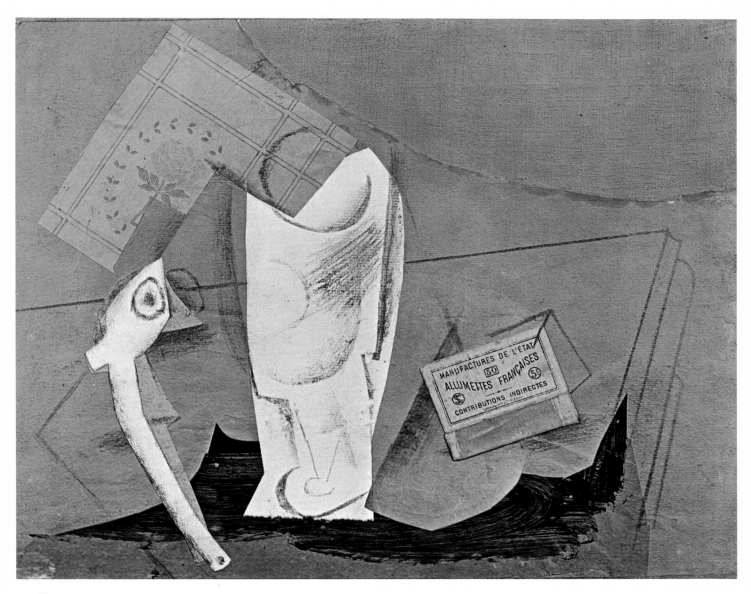

53
Still Life with Pipe, 1913–14, National Gallery, Prague

52
Bottle of Vieux Marc, 1913, National Museum of Modern Art, Paris

54 (ABOVE)
Bottle of Bass, Playing Cards, and Violin, 1914
National Museum of Modern Art, Paris

55 (RIGHT)
Portrait of a Young Girl in Front of a Fireplace, 1914
National Museum of Modern Art, Paris

56 (LEFT)
Harlequin, 1913, Gemeentemuseum
The Hague

57 (RIGHT)
Woman with Guitar, 1914
Emanuel Hoffmann Foundation
Oeffentliche Museum, Basel

59 (ABOVE)
Glass and Pipe, 1918, Justin K. Thannhauser Collection, The Solomon R. Guggenheim Museum, New York

58 (LEFT)
Head of a Man, 1914, private collection

60 (ABOVE)
Still Life, 1919, private collection

61 (RIGHT)
Still Life, 1919, private collection, Paris

62 (LEFT)
Portrait of Olga, 1918
private collection

63 (RIGHT)
*Portrait of Olga in an
Armchair,* 1917
private collection

64 (ABOVE)
Still Life on Bureau, 1919, private collection

65 (RIGHT)
Woman Reading, 1920, private collection

66 (LEFT)
Seated Woman, 1920
private collection

67 (RIGHT)
*Three Women at the
Fountain*, 1921, Museum
of Modern Art, New York

68
Still Life on Fireplace, 1921, National Museum of Modern Art, Paris

69

Guitar, 1920, Emanuel Hoffmann Foundation, Oeffentliche Museum, Basel

70
Three Musicians, 1921, Museum of Modern Art, New York

71
Still Life with Guitar, 1921, Museum of Modern Art, Paris

72
Still Life with Guitar, 1922, M. S. Rosengart, Lucerne

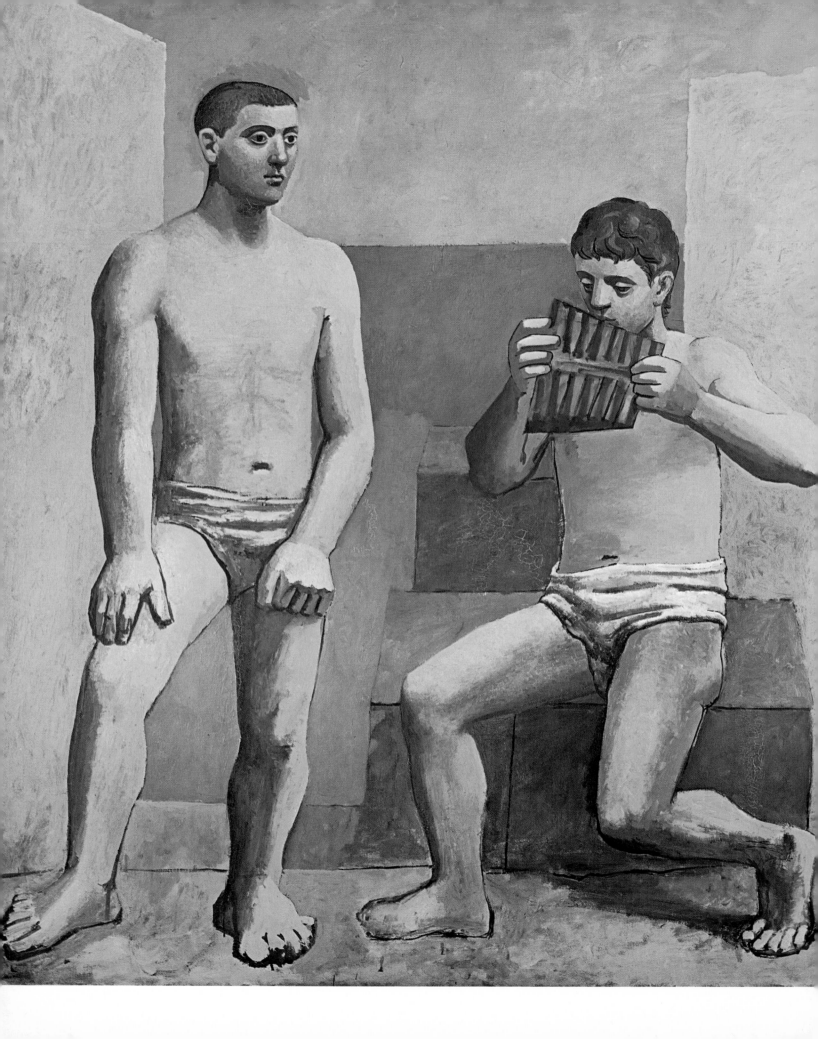

74
Bust of a Woman, 1923, private collection

73
Pipes of Pan, 1923, private collection

75 (ABOVE)
Woman with Blue Veil, 1923, Los Angeles County Museum of Art

76 (RIGHT)
Harlequin, 1923, private collection

77 (ABOVE)
Still Life with Fish, 1923, Mrs. Albert D. Lasker, New York

78 (RIGHT)
The Bird Cage, 1923, Victor W. Ganz, New York

79
Guitar, 1924, Stedelijk Museum, Amsterdam

80
Mandolin and Guitar, 1924, Justin K. Thannhauser Collection
The Solomon R. Guggenheim Museum, New York

82 (ABOVE)
Woman Sculptor, 1925, private collection

81 (LEFT)
Paul as Harlequin, 1924, artist's collection

84 (ABOVE)
Seated Woman, 1927, Museum of Modern Art, New York

83 (LEFT)
The Three Dancers, 1925, Tate Gallery, London

85
The Milliner's Workshop
1926, National Museum
of Modern Art, Paris

86
Seated Woman, 1930, private collection

87
Woman with Pigeons, 1930, National Museum of Modern Art, Paris

88
Crucifixion, 1930, private collection

89
The Rescue, 1937, Beyeler Gallery, Basel

90
Women and Children at Seashore, 1932, Michael Hertz, Bremen

91 (ABOVE)
The Dream, 1932, Victor W. Ganz, New York

92 (RIGHT)
Bather Playing with a Ball, 1932, Victor W. Ganz, New York

93
Bullfight, 1934
Victor W. Ganz, New York

94
Woman with Hat, 1941, Emanuel Hoffmann Foundation, Oeffentliche Museum, Basel

95 (ABOVE)
Interior with Young Girl Drawing, 1935, private collection

96 (BELOW)
The Muse, 1935, National Museum of Modern Art, Paris

98 (ABOVE)
Woman in an Armchair, 1937, artist's collection

97 (LEFT)
Portrait of Dora Maar, 1937, private collection

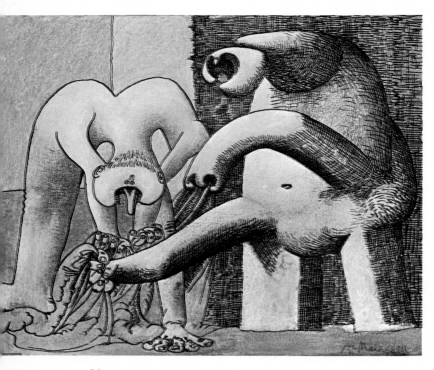

99
Two Nude Women on the Beach, 1937, private collection

100
The Bathers, 1937, private collection

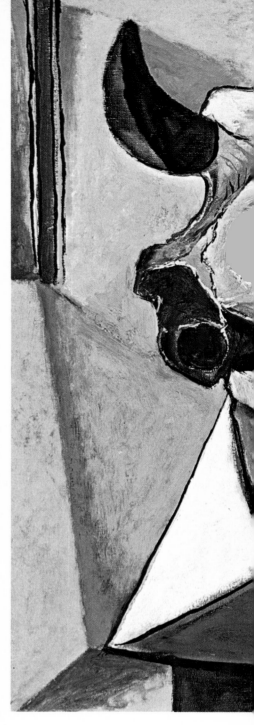

101 (ABOVE LEFT)
Weeping Woman, 1937
R. Penrose, London

102 (LEFT)
Seated Woman, 1938
Norman Granz, Paris

103
Still Life with Fruit and Skull, 1939, private collection

104
Cat Devouring a Bird, 1939, Victor
W. Ganz, New York

105 (OVERLEAF)
Night Fishing at Antibes, 1939
Museum of Modern Art, New York

107
Still Life with Black Bull's Head, 1938, artist's collection

106
Portrait of Maïa with a Doll, 1938, private collection

108 (ABOVE)
Head of Bull in Front of Window, 1942, Jesi, Milan

109 (RIGHT)
Bull's Skull, 1942, private collection

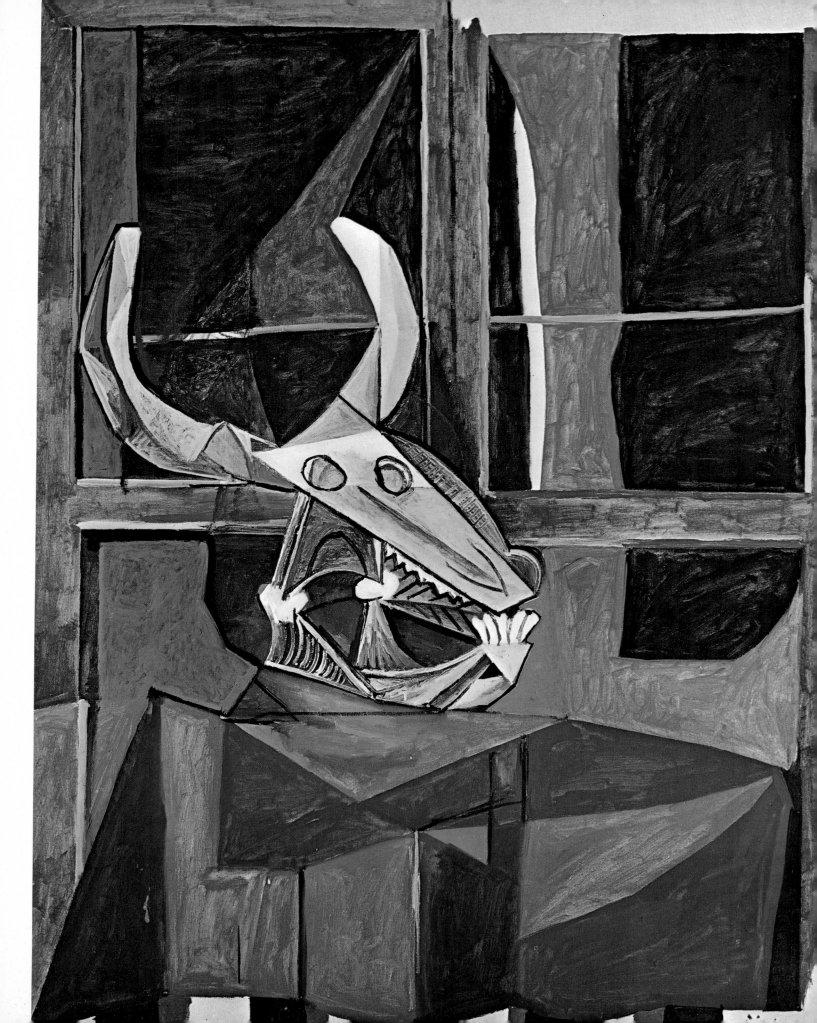

110
Reclining Nude with Musician
(*L'Aubade*), 1942
National Museum of Modern
Art, Paris

111
Woman in Green, 1943, Mr. and Mrs. James Johnson Sweeney, New York

112
Le Vert Galant, 1943, private collection

113
Woman with Hat, 1940–42, Georges Salles, Paris

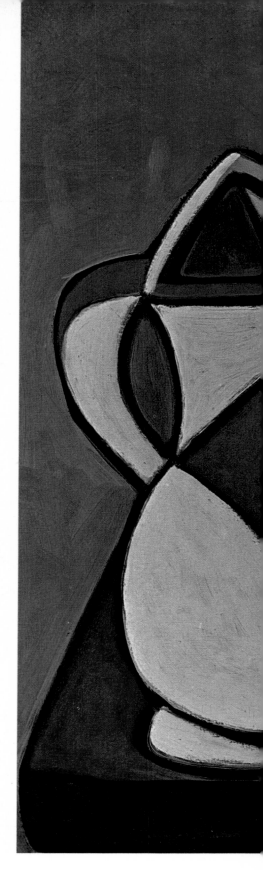

114
Enamel Casserole, 1945, National Museum of Modern Art, Paris

115
The Kitchen, 1946
private collection

116
Figure, 1946, National Museum of Modern Art, Paris

117
Owl and a Chair and Sea Urchins, 1946, Picasso Museum, Antibes

118
La Joie de Vivre, 1946, Picasso Museum, Antibes

119
Les Demoiselles des Bords de la Seine, after Courbet, 1950, Emanuel Hoffmann Foundation, Oeffentliche Museum, Basel

120 (ABOVE LEFT)
Mediterranean Landscape, 1952
private collection

121 (LEFT)
Pages Playing, 1951, private collection

122 (RIGHT)
Portrait of Hélène Parmelin, 1952
private collection

123
War, 1952, Castle Chapel, Vaullauris

124
Peace, 1952, Castle Chapel, Vaullauris

125
Seated Woman in Turkish Costume, 1955, Hamburger Kunsthalle, Hamburg

126
Women of Algiers, after Delacroix, 1955, Victor W. Ganz, New York

127
The Studio at Cannes, 1956, Victor W. Ganz, New York

128–31
Studies for the series *Las Meninas*, 1957, Picasso Museum, Barcelona

132
Le Déjeuner sur l'Herbe (after Manet), 1960, private collection

133
Le Déjeuner sur l'Herbe (after Manet), 1961, M. S. Rosengart, Lucerne

134
Man and Woman, c. 1967
private collection

135
The Watermelon Eater
1967, private collection

138 (ABOVE)
Man and Nude Woman, 1970, private collection

137 (ABOVE LEFT)
Torero (for Jacqueline), 1970, private collection

139 (LEFT)
Couple with Bird, 1970, private collection

136 (OPPOSITE)
Head, 1971, private collection

140 (ABOVE)
Girl Reclining and Reading, polychrome bronze, 1952–55
artist's collection

141 (BELOW)
Head of a Woman, bronze, 1932, private collection

143 (RIGHT)
Monkey with Young, bronze, 1952, private collection

142 (BELOW)
Head of a Faun, bronze, 1949–50, private collection

144
Centaur, bronze, 1948, private collection

COMMENTS AND CRITICISM

Rafael Alberti

I met Pablo Picasso in Paris one evening, when I least expected it, in the orchestra seats at the theater-workshop of Charles Dullin. They were presenting *Rosalinde*, a Jules Supervielle adaption of the Shakespearean text generally known as *As You Like It*.

For some time I had wanted to meet this extraordinary Spaniard from Malaga, this "universal Andalusian" whom our jealous compatriots, in bad faith, considered French, an authentic Parisian product without any ties with his native country because the useless and intolerable monopolizing chauvinism of the French did not acknowledge anything Spanish in him. But I left it to chance and waited for a mere coincidence, influenced no doubt by what "everyone" conceitedly hastened to tell me in order to discourage me, as we sat around the café tables of the Dôme or the Rotonde.

"Picasso is very nice, but he doesn't want to see anyone."

"Nice, Hum! Just ask the painters."

"He's afraid to show what he's painting."

"He's right to do that."

"Perhaps with writers he'd be more polite."

"He's a selfish man."

"You can try to meet him, but it will be difficult."

And during that evening of enchanting Shakesperean forests, with those jealous and unkind comments on the painter still resounding in my ears, I left Supervielle's box where I was sitting, during an intermission, and approached the orchestra seats feeling a little afraid of a chilly greeting, or what would have been even worse, seeing my desire to meet him come to nothing.

"Picasso?"

I must say that he stood up rather diffidently and mechanically, and while he was extending his hand, he fixed his round, grey eyes on me, like two points of unbearable brilliance, animated by a hard and piercing glance. . . . I gave him my name and with faltering voice mentioned some mutual friends and my desire to visit him in his studio.

"Come and see me at 23 Rue La Boétie. But telephone first. Tomorrow, if you can."

The next day, at exactly three in the afternoon, Picasso opened the door of his apartment for me. At first he ushered me into a dark room where suddenly, as he opened the windows, the luxuriant splendor of a *cuadrilla* of seated bullfighters came into view, dressed in flaming silks ranging from the most tempestuous orange to the most violent green. At least this is how they appeared to me though in reality they were the sofa and easy chairs that furnished the room.

Then he took me up to his studio . . . a simple attic with grated window, furnished with a kind of bench entirely covered by books, open or still sealed letters, drawings, pencils. The room was no larger than three by four meters, hardly enough to give the painter space to work at ease. In the center, spread out like a window opening on a precipice, was his current work, one of those amazing productions that pass from his brushes to the canvas in a chaos full of life and poetry.

With his natural, spontaneous courtesy which harshly contradicted the criticisms of the frequenters of the Dôme, Picasso rummaged through the piles of paintings and showed them to me one after the other. The tiny attic then came alive with a disordered dance of line and color, a glittering splendor of striking form, of frenzied genius in an overwhelming, vertiginous avalanche of creativeness.

Yes, an avalanche, like the attack of a powerful Spanish bull released to graze in fiery pastures of poetry, on blood-splashed beaches, or across frozen celestial geometries, like the attack of a bull pulverizing the order of things . . . so as to present it in a new composition, endowed with recreated life, unique and beyond all belief. Then I imagined Picasso nourishing himself with that supernatural pasturage that the Picassian poet from Cordova, Luis de Gongora, offers to the prodigal divinity of his *Solitudini*: the stars.

"First Image of Pablo Picasso," *Europe*, Paris, April-May, 1970

Louis Aragon

To simulate the caning of a chair, Picasso started by placing a piece of paper on his canvas, to which he applied paint at the point where it represented the wood of the chair. But he found it useless to copy laboriously what was already copied, or to copy an object if he could insert the object itself. Also he liked to attach a scrap of old newspaper, add a few lines in charcoal, and that would make up the picture. Extreme, glaring poverty of material always fascinated him. Therein lay the greatness of Cubism at that time—anything, even if it was perishable, would be used by the painters to express themselves, and better still if it was something of no value or something that was actually repelling. Later, people got used to *papiers collés* and insisted on regarding them as studies for future works, or as Picasso told me recently, as "anatom-

Some patrons of the Four Cats, including Père Romeu, far left, Picasso in front of him, and Sabartès at far right

242

ical" models for paintings. Nothing could be more inaccurate. A *papier collé* is an end in itself. Picasso finds it deplorable that painters subsequently painted pictures to simulate the effect of *papier collé*. But its fascination is such that this is not surprising.

La Peinture au Défi, Paris: Corti, 1930

Georges Bataille

The sun, from a human point of view (in the sense, that is, that it merges with the idea of midday), is the most exalted concept possible. Also it is the most abstract, since at midday it is impossible to look at it directly. To complete the metaphor of the sun in the mind of someone who is obliged to avoid it because of the incapacity of his eyes to look at it, the sun, poetically, has the value of mathematical serenity and spiritual elevation. But if, in spite of everything, one insists on looking at it, this indicates a fit of madness and the metaphor changes meaning because the light no longer appears as a productive but as a destructive force, namely combustion. This can be likened from a psychological point of view to the ghastliness of neon light. Actually the sun, fixed in the sky, is identified with mental agitation, with foaming at the lips, with epileptic fits. Just as the sun that can't be looked at is utterly beautiful, the one that is looked at can be considered perfectly hideous. From a mythological point of view, the latter is identified with a man who cuts the throat of a bull (Mithra) or with a vulture who consumes livers (Prometheus); and the one who gazes at it is identified with the slaughtered bull or the eaten liver. . . . It should be added that in mythology the sun has also been identified with a man who slaughters himself, and lastly with an anthropomorphic being without a head. All this leads up to saying that the apex of elevation is related in practice with a sudden fall of incredible violence. The Icarus myth is an excellent example of this: it clearly gives the sun two different attributes—the one that was shining at the moment Icarus was flying up and the one that melted the wax.

This distinction of human attitudes toward two different kinds of sun is especially important because the psychological motives described above are not diverted or weakened by secondary causes. On the other hand, this indicates that it would be *a priori* ridiculous to try to find the exact equivalents of such motives in an activity as complex as painting. It is, however, possible to state that academic painting corresponds more or less to the search for an exaltation of the spirit without excesses. In modern painting, on the contrary, the attempt to break away from extreme exaltation, in a search for dazzling splendor, finds its expression in the elaboration or the decomposition of form; but this is not really felt, strictly speaking, except in Picasso's work.

"Soleil Pourri," Documents, second year, No. 3, Paris, 1930

Cesare Brandi

In psychoanalytical terms, Picasso was the father. The identification with the father had taken place, and there was no longer any rivalry between father and sons. Naturally the sons did not exactly resemble the father, who remained unique and "expert" in his Provençal refuge. This psychological scheme is also at the base of the way Picasso was respected at the end and explains the insistence of the government of Madrid on obtaining *Guernica*.

But it is also for this reason that there is no post-Picasso art now that Picasso is dead. Everything has already happened, everything has already been consumed and burnt out in this happy epoch of "body art" and conceptual art. The only one who survived was Picasso. And he will always survive.

He will survive like a force of nature, like a volcano which is still a volcano even when it is extinct. But not like the ramparts of a city which later become bourgeois boulevards. As long as Picasso's art is popular, even with those who don't understand it, and as long as it has a high investment value, it will never become bourgeois. His strength was not in the contents, which will be recorded as a part of history, but in the sublimity of a formal vision that was, above all, expression. Because of this expressiveness, an epoch has been realized, an epoch that now, with his death, seems finished, although it already came to an end some time ago.

And precisely because of this, his painting is a museum without the trappings of a museum, a permanent patrimony of our culture without being set apart, like a niche in history. Hence his teachings could not be more important: he was not in an ivory tower but on the barricades of his time, and on the right side. And as an artist he was inflexible, one who chose his own language—which was not the language of things but something that lived beyond things and transcending them transformed them—so that he appears to us like an Orpheus who eternally emerges from hell, but without the weakness of turning back.

Corriere della Sera, Milan, October 4, 1973

André Breton

A few days ago, at Picasso's house, I was leafing through the long series of beautiful etchings done recently, which must have meant for him the necessity of taking account, hour by hour, of what properly speaking constitutes for him the meaning and rhythm of his most recent direction. This direction, which is strictly intellectual, is therein deliberately annotated from life. The final delicate veils which, to the eye of the observer, protect artistic creation from complete nudity, fall one by one before this parable of the sculptor. Here we see the artist moving under his legendary, Jovian mask; his penetrating glance goes back and forth from the eternal female model—which he also takes the time to caress—to the block in which are inscribed the infinite possibilities of representation. Or looking outdoors he loses himself in the soft curve of a valley under the sparkle of a clear sky. The eye following with rapture from one engraving to the other—I should say from one state to the other—the infinitely varied spectacle which unfolds on his work table is able to comprehend the stages of the metamorphosis. The heads, which follow one another sheet after sheet—including some that bring to mind the complex

Portrait of André Breton, the leader of the Surrealist movement, for the frontispiece of his book, *Clair de Terre*

revolving lens systems of lighthouses—reveal the secret of their unity, as well as producing amazement at their seeming diversity. This organic, vital unity stands out in comparison to the normality of what goes on next to them and is actually nothing more than simple, very human gestures. A moment ago, the woman's hand was gracefully rising towards his ample beard; now the man raises a small glass bottle containing a fish, holding it up high in his fingers to make it sparkle. Any sense of premeditation is discounted by these charming gestures, typical of all gestures which are a part of life's fascination. It was the point of the graver running over the copper which suddenly dreamt of a new relationship between these two beings and brought in this fish for the enchantment of a few seconds.

A spirit that is so constantly and exclusively inspired can poeticize and ennoble everything. It is made to forcefully oppose and to totally defeat the gloomy designs of those who, for unaccountable reasons, attempt to turn man against himself and to keep him from running away from the anguish that has caused and fostered the idea of dualism. Among the many paintings and objects which Picasso showed me the other day, each more wonderful than the last in their freshness, intelligence, and life, there was one small unfinished canvas . . . with only a large impasto of paint in the center. While making sure that the paint was dry, he explained that the subject of the painting was supposed to be a turd the way it would look after the flies had been chased away. His only regret was that he had had to substitute paint for a real, dried turd—precisely one of those inimitable ones that can be seen in the country during the season when children eat cherries without bothering to spit out the pits. This predilection for pits in this context seemed to me, I must say, to testify in the most objective way to the very special interest which would be appropriate to reserve for the relationship between the assimilated and the nonassimilated, a relationship whose variation, in a positive sense for man, can be considered the essential motivation for artistic creation. The slight repugnance that could have arisen from a consideration of this unique blotch, on which the magic of the painter was just beginning to work, was thus exorcised—and completely so. I found myself imagining the brilliant, newly hatched flies hovering around that Picasso would have known so well how to paint. It was all very cheerful; not only did my eye not remember having rested on anything disagreeable, but I myself was elsewhere, where it was a beautiful day, where it was grand to be alive, amongst wild flowers and dew—and I plunged boldly into the woods.

"Picasso in his Element," *Minotaure*, No. 1, Paris, 1933

Blaise Cendrars

Picasso. I do not know a temperament more tormented, a spirit more restless, or fingers and brushes more rapid and subtle. His impetuosity, his ability, his pride, his equilibrium, his love, cruelty, elegance, and perversity, his design, his arabesque, his rarity, and his acute sense of taste make him a relative of Gilles de Rais [Bluebeard], and both his works and his intellectual order reflect those of a literary man. And this, in painting, is so rare that it is worth while to take note of it. . . . There is neither study [in him], nor imitation of reality, but true absorption. Contemplation. Magnetism and intuition. He is the first liberated painter. He creates. He has a mysterious sense of "correspondences" and knows the secret cipher of the universe. He evokes, he transposes. He denudes enigmatically. He insists. He indicates. . . . He reaffirms life. He adores. He is fascinated. He has no use for scientific analysis, theories of protest, preconceived falsehoods. Rather he possesses unswerving conviction, universal sensitivity, and that stupefying truthfulness of heart. Because he loves, and everything that comes from his hands is always animated.

And above all, he is the painter of reality. Man, animal, plant, unappreciated substances, and subtle abstraction—everything lives, grows, suffers, mates, multiplies, dissappears, moves, keeps growing, menaces, imposes itself, crystallizes. He is the only living being who knows how to paint heat, cold, hunger, thirst, perfume, smell, fatigue, lust, desire, paralysis, palpitations, cramps, and the obscure jolts of the "enormous and delicate" subconscious. At this point his literary demon intervenes. The painter cuts, pierces, saws, stabs, quarters, tears, strangles. Suddenly the substance is there. . . . This gives the key to Picasso's Cubism, which is not purely an esthetic experience as his imitators have believed but rather a kind of religious exorcism which liberates the latent spiritual reality of the world. And again it is love. An ideal transformation. . . .

. . . Like his Harlequins, his painting always has a mask over its face. Too bad for those who have become fascinated by this mystery. Picasso does not want any more disciples. He knows. He is jealous of the face and of the serenity of his painting.

Aujourd'hui, Paris: Grasset, 1931

René Char

Picasso felt at times a prisoner—but a prisoner without a jailer—of the perfect knowledge that gives birth to sadness and melancholy. But never to nostalgia. He loved the painters and gravers of Lascaux, of Altamira, or of any other place where a bull could be found. Even on Velasquez he threw the rosy laughter of amorous license. . . .

As a professional innovator, Picasso amused himself in putting tradition in danger while at the same time using it as a point of departure. Picasso with his encounters and inspirations, Picasso whispering suggestions to Picasso, is revolutionary by nature. Revolutionary. Not terrorist—even in his portraits of chaste love, even when he fixes the image of a personage in a way that the latter hopes to find himself like, in harmony with the beauty that his mirror never reflected and which would unexpectedly dazzle him. Who does not become a clown in his desires? Everyone is confident of his own perfection. Not Picasso. If it is necessary to wait for the disappearance of a great man to learn at what distance from his contemporaries he really lived, we became aware in May, 1973, that Picasso actually lived very close to us.

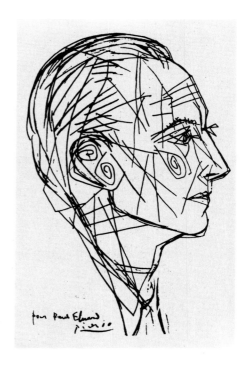

Paul Eluard, poet and close friend

The bird in his recent canvases is the proof of this. But the dates that the painter places so conspicuously on some of his paintings have the prophetic flight of those wild birds which, outlined against the sky, render void the use of the calendar. . . .

Seemingly rather late in life, Picasso displaced the center of gravity of the impudent comedy which goes on interminably around us. But he will not take advantage of this discovery. His "youthfulness" will become wounded and augmented by it. He will rewrite the comedy without mincing matters, neither better nor worse in its general aspects than it is. With regard to the moral wound, however, he will not allow himself to say "So much the worse!" His pugnacious irony, his mad compulsion, and his tellurian inventiveness will be circumscribed momentarily by the ordeal; then, with his unfaltering courage, he will resume the assault. The painted scenes will devour the intrigues and the situations, the characters and the deceptions, until the denouement of the work. . . .

The wizard beguiles, the magician measures. The source of power in Picasso—which has the texture of a dream!—was to liberate the most passionate part of the immanent unknown, ready to rise to the surface in the art of his time and to give it the chance of running its course from falsehood to dream. In this he succeeded. Everything remains possible in the course of time. Picasso's account of it is neither approbation nor condemnation. It must go on. And he proceeds. To impute him with incredible calculation is permissible: pastoral art, magic art, pagan art, undatable art, romanesque art, etc.—art of our eyes. . . .

On the eighth of April, an insistent tomtit tapped his beak seven times against the glass of my window, carrying me suddenly from morning vigilance to midday anxiety. Should I be receiving news? At four o'clock I knew. The awesome eye had ceased to be solar in order to come even closer to us.

Picasso, 1970–1972, catalogue of exhibition
at the Palais des Papes, Avignon, 1973

Jean Cocteau

Here is a Spaniard possessing the oldest French recipes (Chardin, Poussin, Le Nain, Corot) and gifted with magical power. Objects and faces follow him wherever he wants. A dark eye devours them and between the eye through which they enter and the hand by which they leave they are subjected to a rather singular digestive process. Furniture, animals, and people are welded together like lovers. In this metamorphosis none of their objective identity is lost. Picasso changes the natural order of the elements, but he always arrives at the same end.

No sooner does he become aware of his magical power than he makes use of it. What does he experiment on? One recalls Midas when Bacchus gave him the power to change everything he touched into gold. A tree, a column, a statue all intimidate him. He does not dare; he hesitates; he touches some fruit.

Picasso begins with what he finds at hand. A newspaper, a glass, a bottle of anis, an oilcloth, a piece of wallpaper, a pipe, a packet of tobacco, a playing card, a guitar, the cover of a song: "Ma Paloma."

He and Georges Braque, his wizard friend, transmute humble objects. Did they go beyond the studio? We find the source of their harmonies on the Butte Montmartre: neckties in haberdashery shops, imitation marble and faked wood graining on café tables, advertisements for absinthe and *Bass*, soot and wallpaper from houses under demolition, chalk marks on sidewalks for children's games, tobacco-shop signs with the naive representation of a pair of pipes held together with a strip of sky-blue ribbon. . . .

One should see the moment when the tram driver from Malaga nods to a *malagueña* with the tram full of astonished passengers. It is incredible, whether he draws a bullfight in a single flourish without lifting his pen from the page, whether he composes a sculptural poem by folding a thin sheet of tin, or whether in a single night, with the help of the angels, he creates several colossal women, "Junos with cow-like eyes" and large dislocated hands holding cloths of stone.

Dislocated hands? Cow-like eyes? You will say, these women are monsters. It all depends on the use that is made of it. There is a world of difference between intensity of expression and caricature. To anyone who is not aware of this distinction, the Aegina sculptors, Giotto, El Greco, Fouquet, Ingres, Cézanne, Renoir, Matisse, Derain, Braque, and Picasso are caricaturists. . . .

A painter who has nothing but talent . . . possesses only what is necessary. Other more gifted but less solid painters . . . possess extravagance. A painter like Manet combines the two. But rarer still is a rich man with a lot of small change. Picasso adds small change to his wealth. It pours out from his hands and his lips. He speaks? His whimsy reveals his thought in a cruel light. He touches his son's toy? It is no longer a toy. I have seen him kneading a yellow wadded chick from the market while chatting. When he put it back on the table, it had become a Hokusai chick.

At my house, under a glass, I keep a cardboard game die that Picasso once cut out, folded, and painted. I use it to try people out. Whoever ignores this tiny object and claims to like Picasso does not like him for the right reasons.

Where in Picasso does the superfluous end? Where does he begin to reach the essential? It is difficult to say. A complete absence of jesting puts a work done in five minutes on the same plane with something worked over a hundred times. The pleasure of the artist illumines everything and all in the same way. This the professors disapprove of. We are not looking for limits. For Picasso nothing is superfluous, nothing is essential. He knows that this young girl in sepia, in the transparent colors of barley sugar, this tole guitar, and this table in front of a window have equivalent value, that they are worth nothing because he is the mold for them, yet they are worth everything because that mold never repeats the same cast twice, that they deserve a place of honor in the Louvre, and that this will be granted, but that this proves nothing.

Clairvoyance dominates his work. A small spring would be dried up, but

Pencil sketch of Jean Cocteau, avant-garde writer and film maker, done in Rome on Easter Sunday, 1917

for him it preserves his strength and controls the jet. His opulence does not entail any romanticism. His inspiration never overflows. . . . Every work draws on intimate tragedy out of which comes an intense tranquillity. The tragedy does not consist of painting a tiger eating a horse, but in establishing formal relationships between a glass and the molding of an armchair, capable of moving me without recourse to any anecdote.

It is easy to understand the exceptional qualities of subtlety, tact, propriety and pious deception required for such an enormity. Without these qualities the artist would produce a masquerade in which the perspectives make faces, the geometry has a false nose, and bad decorative taste unleashes monsters.

"Between Picasso and Rafiguet,"
Miroirs de l'Art, Paris: Hermann, 1967

Robert Desnos

Truly, the more I think about it, the less I feel capable of genuflecting, and even less, of genuflecting in a group . . . The word "master" burns my lips. I imagine it would also scorch the ears of those to whom it would most legitimately apply and among others, to Picasso.

Everything has been said about him, including what should not have been said. Therefore I don't intend here to contribute to the more or less burlesque parody of his work. That his work resists so much exegesis seems to me already a good reason for admiring it. But, only for reasons of dignity, I would never use those technical expressions, meaningless from overuse, which make it possible to write such precious articles on "touch" and the "symphony of Veronese greens and cobalt blues". . . .

Picasso is an extremely congenial man whom personally I know only slightly, but who always recognizes me when we meet. And this flatters me. I should add that although my shortsightedness often prevents me from recognizing familiar faces, and worse still, makes me greet as perfect strangers friends whom I have seen daily for years, this has never happened to me as far as he is concerned.

I meet Picasso in Paris at only two places: in front of the Saint-Lazare station and in the Jouffroy Passage. . . .

At least I enjoy associating him in my memory with these two places.

The square in front of the Saint-Lazare station is the only place in Paris where I like to drink an apéritif. It seems that between the smells of soot, tar, and gasoline there is the smell of absinthe, of real absinthe. And then, the women in this section are quite special. I keep asking myself why. It is not a question of clothes, of perfume, or of beauty. Seen a hundred yards away, on the Boulevard Haussmann, they would appear just like any other women. But you cannot bring just anyone to the *Critérion* or to the bistros of the Rue Amsterdam. Some people would be terribly out of place there.

Well then? Well, you can draw your own conclusions. But this again makes me think of Picasso. Some of his pictures are marvelous simply because they are his (I insist: because they are his) and would be unacceptable if they were signed by someone else. Yes, signed by someone else.

I don't go by what I hear, you should know that. I always look at the signature of a painting, often before looking at the painting itself. Why? So I won't make a mistake.

And in Picasso's signature there is a kind of graphic magic that plays a very important role in his paintings. Isn't this right? The signature belongs to the painting as much as any other part of it. It is perhaps, it is certainly as important as that blue, yellow, or red. It is even more important. Well, then, Picasso's signature makes me think of the Saint-Lazare district.

But the Jouffroy Passage makes me think of the creator of *Les Demoiselles d'Avignon*, for other reasons. This thoroughfare is filled with the smell of perfume, of leather, of linen being ironed. It is made up of all the elements of the street, it epitomizes them, it is the people, it is Parisian. It has the accent of Belleville or of the Rue Mouffetard. Here one feels at home. And without doubt it is this sense of ease and well-being that strikes me when I meet Picasso in that locality where someone, I don't remember who, once noticed a poster advertising a lotion: a stout woman in blue, seen full-face. He asserted that years before becoming acquainted with the stout women painted by Picasso, this corner of Paris would irresistibly make him think of the painter.

I am not joking. What I have just said about this artist, which is more or less everything that I know about him . . . tells me more about his work than the most subtle theories of Messrs. X, Y, or Z.

"Bonjour M. Picasso," *Documents*, second year, No. 3, Paris, 1930

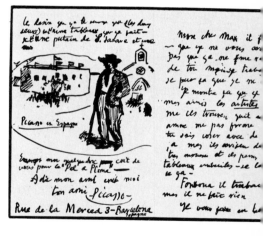

Ilya Ehrenburg

At the beginning of 1915, Picasso took me to his studio which was not far from the Rotonde, on the Rue Schoelcher. . . . There was no room to turn around. Canvases, cardboard sheets, pieces of tin, iron wire, and pieces of wood were all over the place. The tubes of paint took up one whole corner. I have never seen so many, even in a shop. Picasso explained that having often found himself unable to buy any because he didn't have the money and having just sold several paintings, he had decided to stock up "for life." Everything was painted—the walls, the cigar boxes, a broken stool. He said he couldn't bear to see a surface without color.

He was then thirty-four years old, but seemed younger with his incredibly black, penetrating, lively eyes, his black hair and his small, almost feminine hands. At the Rotonde he was often gloomy and taciturn. But there were moments when he abandoned himself to gaiety and joked to the point of irritating his friends. He seemed uneasy, and this uneasiness soothed me. I understood, as I looked at him, that my feeling was not a unique reaction, or a weakness, but the peculiarity of an epoch. I have already said that Picasso was often dear to me for the destructive quality he had in him. In that light I knew and loved him during the war of 1914. Many insist that he was then indifferent to what is termed politics. If this word means the changing of ministers or the polemics in the newspapers, it is true that Picasso turns to the comics in *Le Matin* rather than the official communiqués.

But I remember the joy with which he received the news of the Russian Revolution in February. On that occasion he gave me one of his canvases. . . .

One has to have a lot of bad faith, ignorance, or naïveté to construe Picasso's long and difficult career as a love for originality at all costs, the desire to *épater le bourgeois* or the cult of "isms." Picasso often remarked that he finds it ridiculous that people say he is looking for new forms: "I only look for one thing—to express what I want. I am not looking for new forms—I find them."

One day he confessed to me that when he sets to work, he does not always know whether it will be a Cubist painting or something entirely realistic. He is guided by the model and his own humor.

A young and attractive American girl had posed for him at Vallauris, and Picasso did a dozen drawings and oil sketches of her. In the first version, the girl was exactly as everyone saw her . . . . Then little by little Picasso began to penetrate the enigma of her face. Undoubtedly something different than her angelic appearance had been revealed to him. . . . At a showing of his works, someone next to me who was standing in front of the tenth version of the portrait thought it witty to exclaim: "Look, a pig in cubes!"

The person had no idea that another portrait of the same girl, which had a few moments before aroused his complete admiration, was the first stage in the formation of that Cubist porcine likeness. . . .

Contradictions in Picasso? They certainly exist. Some people like to say: "The work of Picasso is all a contradiction." But remember the dates. Picasso started to exhibit in 1901 and now, as I write these lines, it is already the end of 1961. Have there not perhaps been contradictions in the world in these sixty years? Picasso did not live in the past nor in the future. He expressed the complexity, the loss, and the desperation of his time; also the hope. He has torn apart and he has built. He loves and he hates.

I have been lucky enough to know some of the men who have made their imprint on the physiognomy of this century. I have seen not only the tempest and the fog, but also the human figures, and I consider that spring day long ago when I met Picasso for the first time one of the most auspicious moments of my life.

"Remembrances of Pablo Picasso,"
La Nouvelle Critique, No. 130, Paris, November, 1961

Max Jacob

When he came to Paris, Picasso led the rowdy existence of apprentices. Thanks to the son of a prominent functionary in the Museum of Natural History, he and some other Spaniards would come by night to the Jardin des Plantes to see the animals. He frequented the Moulin-Rouge, the Casino of Paris, and other then popular music halls. He met fashionable ladies: Liane de Pugny, the beautiful Otero, and Jeanne Bloch, and he drew rather good likenesses of them.

He wore a top hat that he later gave to me and that was, indeed, magnificent; for although he always liked simple clothes which he bought in coopera-

Left above: drawing in a 1902 letter from Picasso to Max Jacob; left below, Picasso, Jacob, and their cat in Paris, 1905; above, Jacob in 1917

tive stores, this was an extreme form of refinement: he is extremely fastidious and chooses drawers to match his socks with as much care as he paints a picture. . . .

At that time I was an art critic. I expressed my admiration and was invited to meet him by a certain Mr. Mañach who knew French and who was managing all this eighteen-year-old boy's affairs.

I went to see them, Mañach and Picasso; I spent a day looking at hundreds of paintings! He did one or two every day, or at night, and sold them for 150 francs.

Picasso did not know French and I was ignorant of Spanish, but we looked at each other and shook hands enthusiastically. We were in a huge studio in the Place Clichy, where Spaniards sat on the floor, eating and talking gaily. . . . The next day they all came to see me and Picasso painted a portrait of me on a huge canvas which has since been lost or reused for another painting. In the portrait I was sitting on the floor amidst my books, in front of a large fire. . . .

The art dealers who now boast of having discovered Picasso all considered him crazy at that time (around 1905). "Your friend is mad!" Mr. V . . . told me. One day Picasso was ill and I went to offer to sell one of his landscapes to this same Mr. V. He said to me in disdain, "The bell tower is crooked!" and shrugged his shoulders.

Picasso offered drawings for tenpence to a mattress shop on the Rue des Martyrs, and those ten pennies were accepted with gratitude.

In the evenings we would give plays by the light of a kerosene lamp, since we could not afford to go to other people's plays. We took turns taking all the parts, including that of scene director, producer, electrician and technician, and made these personages take part in the play as well. (Pirandello did not invent anything new.) We knew a restaurant which would give us credit and then later we would always pay. We would then bring all our friends, and the restaurant, if it was not rich, was always full. . . .

For a while, several of us would go to Matisse's for dinner on Thursday evenings—Picasso, André Salmon, Apollinaire, and myself. I think it was at Matisse's that Picasso first saw African sculpture, or at least it was there that he became captivated by it. He never confided to me anything about the invention of Cubism. I am therefore reduced to the hypothesis, and no one can stop me from stating it, that Cubism was born from African sculpture. Picasso began to draw large figures with their noses attached to their eyes (1906 or 1907). He immersed himself in deep meditation, simplifying animals and things and finally arriving at drawings executed with a single stroke that recall those in prehistoric caves. I doubt whether there are any of these still in existence. He would say to us: "Go and enjoy yourselves!" At that time, besides, he began to suffer from a kidney disease which for ten years forced him to a horribly strict diet—limited to spaghetti without salt or pepper. His wonderful stoicism reflects the whole life, character, and soul of this man whose equal I have yet to see.

"Remembrances of Picasso," *Cahiers d'Art*, No. 6, Paris, 1927

The Madman, 1904

Marcel Jouhandeau

This evening I went down beneath the Pont Neuf to see a man who believes he is God-the-Father. The same cut of beard, the same general bearing. They had told me he was mad. Was he fooling me? He was nude, or almost nude, under a green scarf, and declared to me: "Here is my radio transmitter. I have just communicated with the four corners of the world. They throw stones at me from the parapet but those who throw them at me cannot reach me. The Angels sitting on that plane tree are fending the blows with a racquet. I have warehouses all over the world. I know that the astrakhans I bought in Russia are getting moldy, but it doesn't matter; they will repair them, and if it is necessary to replace all the skins, one by one, it will be done. My vaults on the Rue du Bac are so damp. Ah! I also have three barges of fruits and vegetables on the Seine. A banana is like an egg. An egg? You touch it, and it breaks. A banana? You touch it, and it spoils. And my melons? My beloved Son is busy buying them in the south. At this moment he is in Rome with the Pope. It is like the Théâtre du Châtelet (he points it out), I have the general supervision of it. Well sir, you cannot imagine what a job that is."

While God was talking I looked around his house without walls, roof, door, or window, where everything was in good order in the open air around a single tree: the linen, the chests, the umbrella tied with twine at both ends, some platters, some colanders connected with a piece of wire fastened at the other end to a huge stove. But this wasn't, as one might think, the kitchen equipment—it was the radio transmitter.

Underneath the bridge was the wardrobe. I noticed a pilgrim's cross in the buttonhole of a jacket. "What is this?" I asked. "Are you a devout man?" "No, sir. Look at that other coat with the tricolor cockade, and the third has a red immortelle. I belong to all religions. According to whom I have to deal with, Peter, Paul, or James, I change my coat. I have ten of them. I should have a hundred. For you, I know very well which I should put on, but you don't know which one to put on for me. However, foreseeing your visit, I preferred to remain nude. This was another way of pleasing you. Don't therefore think that I am deceived by your compliments. It is you who are deceived by me and mine, or we are both deceived if you are the Devil. In the meantime, this evening I will leave, and it will be very difficult for you ever to find God-the-Father again."

"God-the-Father," *Documents*, second year, No. 3, Paris, 1930

Michel Leiris

The world transformed into a furnished hotel room where everyone is flinging his arms around awaiting death; the sun reduced to the dimensions of an electric light shining two fingers away from our heads in sordid intimacy; the agony of the horse twisted like a Pegasus suddenly caught in some frightful den; the bull—the sole victor—everlastingly darting his horns; the people convulsed; the hard table; the bird shrieking itself hoarse: it is useless to look for words to describe this epitome of our black and white catastrophe—the life we live like pawns on a chessboard that would be capable of feeling all the hostile relationships between them, like so many knives, subject to the royal pleasure of the players, without their tremors of pain being able to deflect one iota the rules of a savage geometry.

To take a pen and put down words as if one could add something to Picasso's *Guernica* is, of all tasks, the most presumptuous. In a black and white rectangle, such as this ancient tragedy appears to us in, Picasso sends us our mourning card: everything that we love is about to die, and this is why it is necessary that everything we love be summarized in something of ineffable beauty, like an effusion of final good-byes.

Just as the cry of the *cante hondo* has to wait until it reaches the throat of the singer before it can transform its calamitous, earthy quality into a mother-of-pearl iridescence, so do the black and white exhalations become crystallized through Picasso's hands and take on the sparkle of diamonds, exhalations that are the breath of a world in agony which the most hideous meteors—knives of our ambition—are preparing to cut to the bone.

"Participation," Cahiers d'Art, No. 4-5, Paris, 1937

Pierre MacOrlan

My image of this great painter who was also a great giver of life is that of a short, thick-set young man whose sparkling eyes seemed to me worthy of envy and wonder. He wore blue overalls like a mechanic. But he seemed more like a prince dressed as a mechanic, not in order to be incognito but to feel at ease. In short, he clearly dominated his group, perhaps also because he bore the mysterious and awe-inspiring mark of fortune. . . .

He arrived from Barcelona. He had learned to bestow on poverty a kind of contagious poetic quality concentrated in those extraordinary Rose and Blue periods, which broke all literary and artistic traditions for exploiting misery. Everything became rose and blue and angelic in this world of misery, whether in the shade or in the sun, because Picasso wanted his vagabonds, his acrobats, his gypsies, his masked figures, and the young girls offstage to be dressed in rose and blue. Altogether, it is he who best represents that period before the war, during those years when the world was preparing for the debacle. It was a period of hasty and negligent intelligence that portended the destiny of those who lived in it.

Picasso is a force fed by presentiment and it is difficult to limit the radiating capacity of that force. I don't know how he lives today—probably seated on a golden throne like the free-thinking popes. But now, as I write, he reappears at my house, wearing a blue overall like the one he wore twenty years ago, twenty inconceivably short years.

"Meeting Picasso,"
Les Annales Politiques et Littéraires, No. 2338, July 15, 1929

Jacques Maritain

A lifework such as Picasso's represents for painting a tremendous advance in self-realization. His example is as meaningful to a philosopher as to an artist, so that even a philosopher can comment on it from his point of view.

In order to find a pure expression which is free from human interference and that kind of "literature" which arises from pride of eye and its acquired capacity, Picasso exerts a heroic strength of will and boldly confronts the unknown. His painting then makes a step forward towards its mystery. At every moment he grazes on the sin of beatifying. Anyone else, at those heights, would fall. I imagine that by dint of subjecting painting to itself and its own purely formal laws, he begins to feel it failing under his hand, and that then becoming filled with rage, he seizes the first thing that comes to hand and fixes it to the wall with infallible sensibility. But he is always saved because he endows everything he touches with an incomparable poetic richness.

Picasso has this contact with poetry because he is completely a painter. In this he is in the tradition of the great masters and recalls one of their most useful lessons. It has been rightfully observed that his works do not despise reality, they *resemble* it, with that spiritual resemblance—surrealistic, to use a profoundly true word—which I have already spoken of. Whether dictated by demon or angel, one hesitates at times to judge. But not only are things transfigured when they pass from his eye to his hand, there is another mystery which simultaneously comes into play. The soul and flesh of the painter are seeking to substitute themselves for the objects he is painting, trying to discharge their essence, to enter and offer themselves under the mask of the very things represented in the painting, where they can live an independent life, different from their own.

Cahiers d'Art, No. 3-5, Paris, 1932

Alberto Moravia

Some time ago I wrote a small essay on Picasso's Rose and Blue periods. Among other things I said that with Picasso's painting the century began exactly as it should then proceed and as now it is proceeding—with art building on art, an art that is no longer taken directly from reality but mediated by estheticism, an art taken away from critical conscience and from the tempest of creativity towards the quiet lagoons of mannerism, and then later, of destruction.

What did I mean by these words? At least five things: 1) that mannerism is a way of creating art and that it does not come directly from reality but from art itself; 2) that Picasso was a great mannerist, the greatest perhaps of all times; 3) that mannerism in art is the syncretism of religion and the technology in science; 4) that Picasso, great, pleasing, and mannerist, reveals himself as the true painter of a syncretist and technological epoch which recognizes the rule of the masses; 5) finally, that from the moment that life and work are identified with each other within Picasso, one can say that Picasso worked all his life for his true public who were the masses, and that, therefore, his political commitment, even according to his own words, was the logical consequence of all his work.

Someone might object at this point that Picasso's public, that is, the

Guillaume Apollinaire with his head bandaged from a World War I wound

people who buy his paintings, are all very rich and therefore it is difficult to see them as "leftist." I would reply that yes they are very rich; but from a cultural point of view, which is really the only one that counts in the appreciation of art, they form a part of the masses like everyone else. Culture today, in fact, is encyclopedic, syncretistic, popularized, Alexandrian, and eclectic. Thus the culture of the rich is the culture of the poor.

Someone else might say: but Picasso was a relentless experimenter, one of the protagonists of the historic avant-garde. Certainly. But the historic avant-garde is one of the more showy aspects of the lapse of art into a kind of critical-popularizing exploitation which is practiced by the museums. A slipping towards art that talks about art. Towards art that has nothing to say but a lot to give. In the paintings of Picasso there aren't any objects to which the painter feels an irresistible attraction, as, for example, Van Gogh's wicker chair. What attracts Picasso is the fact that others before him were attracted by the object and painted it. The objects then, in him, are removed from their original reality. They are second or even third-hand objects: the bulls in Goya, the nudes on Greek vases, or African masks.

Picasso therefore was the painter par excellence of an epoch of the masses. This does not so much justify his political commitment as explain it (the historical motives are obvious: from the war in Spain to the horrors of Nazism, from revolution in the 'Twenties to counterrevolution in the 'Thirties).

Corriere della Sera, Milan, November 4, 1973

A 1922 pencil sketch of Léon Bakst, who was a scene designer for Diaghilev

Jacques Prévert
Attention!
The welcome mat is spread out before the door of the studio and there they all are wallowing, shouting their admiration and mewing their enthusiasm.

With eyes closed and supported by their intellectual crutches, they settle down in front of the grotto awaiting miracles, equipped with a pen full of the viscous water of "pictorial problems."

Soon they are pushing and biting each other, rummaging through the records, throwing boxes of dates at each other and searching for new metaphors in the sweepings of the artist and the rose harlequins of his youthful repasts. The cleverest and most insipid slip through the door, stay a while, and then rush off to swap sketches for checks. . . .

Those who don't like that kind of painting also come . . . ; they thought they had heard the Sicilian Vespers of modern painting being sounded at the Louvre and came with their *Sunsets in Provence* to sign up at the Office of Tears, on the Street of Weeping Willows. There ensues a confrontation, a fray, and a great fight of octopuses hurling black clouds of ink at each other.

The canvases are no longer visible.

Alone in his studio Picasso looks at the clock, whistles twice through his fingers, the genius of painting enters on tiptoe and the act begins. . . .

He works. But outside can be heard the hissing of the critic's darts, the

Portrait de Pierre Reverdy, done as a frontispiece for his book, *Cravates de Chanvre*, 1922

sinister chanting of the connoisseurs and the creators of books . . . those who love, understand, predict, foresee, and explain so well and smell so bad. . . .

To quell the throng of these professional admirers, the painter throws everything that comes to hand across the threshold of his studio, things that he wants to show, drawings done in an idle moment, and beautiful paintings, canvases that are lively, scintillating, and recent—very recent.

And then they go away, back to their houses and galleries like moles, where they bleat and sing and invite others in to see.

They offer pastries, but some blithe spirit, someone who is jealous for certain and is hiding behind a curtain, insinuates softly: "It's not a Picasso."

The refined and select company turns acid, their common saliva stalls the engine, the fan stops, and a few ladies make the sign of the cross. Picasso did not sign it!

A choked voice asks: "Is there an expert in the room?" There is one. He approaches the canvas, sniffs the back, picks at it like a dog scratching a bone, and with strange sounds in his mouth he announces: "It's a Picasso."

The fan starts up again, the pastries are passed around, but the expert continues: "It's a Picasso, but it is fake, and yet it is certainly he who did it in spite of everything, there's no doubt."

Everyone rushes to the cloakroom, demoralized. Outside it is night and it is raining.

With his bowler hat firmly fixed on his head Picasso, the lord of painting, like a Fantômas of terror with one foot on the right bank, one on the left, and the third behind the imbeciles, stands watching the Seine flowing down from Mt. Junkheap when he would like to be visiting the castles on the Loire.

"Homage—Homage," *Documents*, second year, No. 3, Paris, 1930

Pierre Reverdy

Who, in that interminable and ceaseless struggle, could have had a greater right than he to maintain that he had shown the greatest perseverance, audacity, and courage?

From the first day he was prey to every attack, every insult, and every kind of slander. Even in the best moments of this incredible adventure . . . he made many uncompromising enemies.

Yet this was only the most prestigious and alluring aspect of the challenge. On another side, in the gloomy depths of the abyss, this man was reduced in time and space to his narrowest limits and tormented by the depth of his genius, because genius is perhaps the drama of the greatest depth—the purest and most lucid consciousness of depth, the depth of conscience—joined with the most alive, the most active, and the most avid intellectual and sensual faculties. From this is born that hunger which seeks to absorb in youth everything that falls beneath the eyes, hands, and teeth. Whence that need to torture others and oneself in that exclusive search for means that will make it possible to free the personality trapped in its gangue, extract it out of the chaos which is suffocating it, and lift it up to the light of mastery.

It is a question of moving on and changing flags in the game of domination.

In any case, the man has chosen before he leaves.

Not having been born to be a victim, he will be an executioner.

But what the predestined doesn't realize immediately is that this alternative forces him to become his own executioner as well as and perhaps more than that of others and that everything that will accrue to him in life, everything that will give nourishment to his work, will not suffice to satisfy his avidity of soul nor his hunger, because nothing that he could be or possess could have enough value or enough savor not to remain extraneous to him—nothing, that is, except his work which will devour him because it is more important than he. Then he can only live for glory, and only his work can give him that glory, and only that will permit him to rise above the common measure of human limits in space and time.

Then the work becomes more and more exacting. It allows no distraction without provoking remorse. Only by working frantically and producing stubbornly can he find any kind of relief. Without this, a deadly boredom fills his world.

Not finding peace within himself, he cannot bear to see it in others, and he does not rest until he has pulled them into his torment. Having once achieved glory and conquered fortune, everything that the world can offer is within reach of his hands, but at the same time the deepest moral misery is close at hand. His soul is devoured by the fire of ambition, and to quell that feeling of emptiness, that bare world with nothing worth the effort of loving, then he must fill it with himself, because everything that can be obtained from it, far from satisfying him, pushes him back towards himself, towards the frenetic desire to fill everything in this life and in eternity with himself.

Serge Diaghilev and Salisburg, a lawyer, about 1919

But time has ripened. Now a thick carpet of green leaves is spread on the earth, exhaling a suffocating cloud. They are laurel leaves and the perfume is too intoxicating, too strong. We have come down slowly from the solitary heights where the air is always fresh and pure, down into the infernal circle where the nauseating, obscene appetite of renown holds sway, giving us the shame and disgust of the human state almost to the point of vomiting. It's a shame, because, in any other sense, man also has matured and he has justly profited by the immense success due to the artist. . . .

Because of this I still happen to see, almost without my being aware of it . . . between two sharp peaks on the far horizon, the vision of a gigantic medallion surrounded by the heads of hunters and dogs and, right in the center, looking grave and somber under a blinding light, the figure of this man to whom has been promised the glory of all time, and who finds himself, in this his highest moment, to be a marked man, a tree to be felled. And yet he has somehow managed to remain splendidly on his feet—the image of my dear friend.

"An Eye of Light and of Night,"
Le Point, XLI, Souillac, April, 1952

258

Georges Ribémont-Dessaignes

Painting has had a strange destiny. Thrown as nourishment for the worst exigencies of man, while at the beginning it was a flight of the spirit, it has managed to rove about for centuries and centuries in an atmosphere of cuisine, with rises and falls, amid meanness, adulation, base falsehoods and thousands of manias, one of the most disgusting of which is, without doubt, the desire to flatten the world. But suddenly, when one has come to believe that painting is entirely absorbed in the business of appearances, it gives a vigorous shake of the reins and, under some reflection of a sun high up in the domain of the ideal, it presents a human face and reestablishes itself to the point of making us almost forget its past wretchedness and making us believe that only its present greatness is valid. It is enough that Picasso lives, so that painting, all painting, ceases to be an art of the blind and the decapitated. You understand surely what I mean. The eye of the painter is an organ without much importance, enamored of its own vices within its moist orbit. The astonishing power to conceive and behold, is something else. When this "something else" reveals itself with the dazzling diversity of Picasso, then man can begin to have faith in himself. . . .

Nothing of what can be said about Picasso is exact, and never can be. To describe even a minimum part may be one of those pastimes dear to scholars whose prime virtue is to predict death. But it is a useless and vain labor. There are those who, full of courage, dare to add one part to another in the hope of creating a wide range—the widest range possible—for Picasso. They have hardly completed their analysis before the matter overflows with a new creation harsher or more caressing than the others. Then the critic feels stifled and starts to cough convulsively. What would happen if he were forced to realize that there is still within Picasso everything that he has not yet produced, things that he cannot guess at and of which he hasn't the least idea? It is exactly in this, it seems, that the phenomenal side of Picasso's genius lies. He comprises everything that men have created, but he teaches them how to make use of it. He takes their toys and brings them to life. But what a life! Is he himself the master of it once the enchantment is over? It would seem that he is.

I speak with good reason of enchantment. Here it is not a question of representation but the practice of magic when the magic is an action of man on nature. Within the precise limits given by the four angles of the frame, a painting by Picasso entraps external elements that are noted and at hand every second of our life, yet which always escape us, rebellious behind a familiar grin. Taken by surprise, in vain they proclaim their independence and appeal to some obscure or astonishing paternity. But they remain trapped and for eternity we will be witnesses of their stern voices or of their rage. The eyes of family portraits which penetrate and follow you implacably, wherever you move, do not have the same insistence and do not express the same hidden life. I know someone who, to preserve his equanimity, only looks at those portraits through the opening of a keyhole. The portraits still gaze at him in spite of his precautions. Probably, the paintings of Picasso also look

Igor Stravinsky, 1920

at you through keyholes. And I don't believe there is another painter today whose works have that power.

"Picasso as Meteor," *Documents*, second year, No. 3, Paris, 1930

Gualtieri di San Lazzaro

. . . We have lost in Picasso our sovereign, our chief, and our protector. The King is dead. But he will be succeeded by no other king in the great republic of bizarre bureaucrats and triumphant upstarts.

During the Occupation it was he who took us to the bistro and then to the Café de Flore. His dog, Fiston, was still alive; Picasso had difficulty feeding him and, especially, keeping him warm. Our King did not consider himself defeated. He was ever "ready to challenge all the German painters on a large public square," he said, adding: "Why not Piazza San Marco, in Venice?" One had to be home before the curfew. I can still see the church of Saint-Germain-des-Prés bathed in a soft silvery light. "Why not here," Picasso insisted, "there's a fabulous moonlight." In those moments there was something marvelously childish in his genius. "I am always fourteen years old," he told his dealer and biographer D. H. Kahnweiler. . . .

Eugène d'Ors . . . said that the genius of Picasso was more Italian than Spanish or French. Even today this seems to me an acceptable opinion. But in his castles, in his villas on the Côte d'Azur, and in his Paris apartments, despite the doves circling around him with their white wings, as if he were a god of love, he only led the life of a middle-class Frenchman, or better still, of a workman. By asking to be buried at Vauvenargues, he ended his existence in Spanish style, in the inviolate grandeur of solitude.

He was against Franco because of his crimes, but especially because he had deprived him of his greatest love—deep down in his heart he always loved only Spain.

"Mort d'un Roi," *Vingtième Siècle*, No. 40, Paris, June, 1973

Gertrude Stein

We went up a couple of steps and through the open door passing on our left the studio in which later Juan Gris was to live out his martyrdom but where then lived a certain Vaillant, a nondescript painter who was to lend his studio as a ladies dressing room at the famous banquet for Rousseau, and then we passed a steep flight of steps leading down where Max Jacob had a studio a little later, and we passed another steep little stairway which led to the studio where not long before a young fellow had committed suicide, Picasso painted one of the most wonderful of his early pictures of the friends gathered round the coffin, we passed all this to a larger door where Gertrude Stein knocked and Picasso opened the door and we went in.

He was dressed in what the french call the singe or monkey costume, overalls made of blue jean or brown, I think his was blue and it is called a singe or monkey because being all of one piece with a belt, if the belt is not fastened, and it very often is not, it hangs down behind and so makes a monkey. His eyes were more wonderful than even I remembered, so full and

Four of Picasso's friends in his apartment on the Rue La Boétie, 1919: Jean Cocteau, Olga Koklova Picasso, Erik Satie, and Clive Bell

so brown, and his hands so dark and delicate and alert. We went further in. There was a couch in one corner, a very small stove that did for cooking and heating in the corner, some chairs, the large broken one Gertrude Stein sat in when she was painted and a general smell of dog and paint and there was a big dog there and Picasso moved her about from one place to another exactly as if the dog had been a large piece of furniture. He asked us to sit down but as all the chairs were full we all stood up and stood until we left. It was my first experience of standing but afterwards I found that they all stood that way for hours. Against the wall was an enormous picture, a strange picture of light and dark colors, that is all I can say, of a group, an enormous group and next to it another in a sort of a red brown, of three women, square and posturing, all of it rather frightening. Picasso and Gertrude Stein stood together talking. I stood back and looked. I cannot say I realised anything but I felt that there was something painful and beautiful there and oppressive but imprisoned. I heard Gertrude Stein say, and mine. Picasso thereupon brought out a smaller picture, a rather unfinished thing that could not finish, very pale almost white, two figures, they were all there but very unfinished and not finishable. Picasso said, but he will never accept it. Yes, I know, answered Gertrude Stein. But just the same it is the only one in which it is all there. Yes, I know, he replied and they fell silent. After that they continued a low toned conversation and then Miss Stein said, well, we have to go, we are going to have tea with Fernande. Yes, I know, replied Picasso. How often do you see her, she said, he got very red and looked sheepish. I have never been there, he said resentfully. She chuckled, well anyway we are going there, she said, and Miss Toklas is going to have lessons in french. Ah the Miss Toklas, he said, with small feet like a Spanish woman and earrings like a gypsy and a father who is king of Poland like the Poniatowskis, of course she will take lessons. We all laughed and went to the door. There stood a very beautiful man, Oh Agero, said Picasso, you know the ladies. He looks like a Greco, I said in english. Picasso caught the name, a false Greco, he said. Oh I forgot to give you these, said Gertrude Stein, handing Picasso a package of newspapers, they will console you. He opened them up, they were the Sunday supplement of american papers, they were the Katzenjammer kids. Oh oui, Oh oui, he said, his face full of satisfaction, merci thanks Gertrude, and we left.

We left then and continued to climb higher up the hill. What did you think of what you saw, asked Miss Stein. Well, I did see something. Sure you did, she said, but did you see what it had to do with those two pictures you sat in front of so long at the vernissage. Only that Picassos were rather awful and the others were not. Sure, she said, as Pablo once remarked, when you make a thing, it is so complicated making it that it is bound to be ugly, but those that do it after you they don't have to worry about making it and they can make it pretty, and so everybody can like it. . . .

It was only a very short time after this that Picasso began the portrait of Gertrude Stein, now so widely known, but just how that came about is a little vague in everybody's mind. I have heard Picasso and Gertrude Stein talk about it often and they neither of them can remember. They can remember the first time that Picasso dined at the rue de Fleurus and they can remember the first time Gertrude Stein posed for her portrait at rue Ravignan but in between there is a blank. How it came about they do not know. Picasso had never had anybody pose for him since he was sixteen years old, he was then twenty-four and Gertrude Stein had never thought of having her portrait painted, and they do not either of them know how it came about. Anyway it did and she posed to him for this portrait ninety times and a great deal happened during that time. To go back to all the first times.

Picasso and Fernande came to dinner, Picasso in those days was, what a dear friend and schoolmate of mine, Nellie Jacot, called, a good-looking bootblack. He was thin, dark, alive with big pools of eyes and a violent but not a rough way. He was sitting next to Gertrude Stein at dinner and she took up a piece of bread. This, said Picasso, snatching it back with violence, this piece of bread is mine. She laughed and he looked sheepish. That was the beginning of their intimacy.

That evening Gertrude Stein's brother took out portfolio after portfolio of japanese prints to show Picasso, Gertrude Stein's brother was fond of japanese prints. Picasso solemnly and obediently looked at print after print and listened to the descriptions. He said under his breath to Gertrude Stein, he is very nice, your brother, but like all americans, like Haviland, he shows you japanese prints. Moi j'aime pas ca, no I don't care for it. As I say Gertrude Stein and Pablo Picasso immediately understood each other.

Then there was the first time of posing. The atelier of Picasso I have already described. In those days there was even more disorder, more coming and going, more red-hot fire in the stove, more cooking and more interruptions. There was a large broken armchair where Gertrude Stein posed. There was a couch where everybody sat and slept. There was a little kitchen chair upon which Picasso sat to paint, there was a large easel and there were many very large canvases. It was at the height of the end of the Harlequin period when the canvases were enormous, the figures also, and the groups.

There was a little fox terrier there that had something the matter with it and had been and was again about to be taken to the veterinary. No frenchman or frenchwoman is so poor or so careless or so avaricious but that they can and do constantly take their pet to the vet.

Leo Stein

Fernande was as always, very large, very beautiful and very gracious. She offered to read La Fontaine's stories aloud to amuse Gertrude Stein while Gertrude Stein posed. She took her pose, Picasso sat very tight on his chair and very close to his canvas and on a very small palette which was of a uniform brown grey color, mixed some more brown grey and the painting began. This was the first of some eighty or ninety sittings.

Toward the end of the afternoon Gertrude Stein's two brothers and her sister-in-law and Andrew Green came to see. They were all excited at the beauty of the sketch and Andrew Green begged and begged that it should be left as it was. But Picasso shook his head and said, non.

It is too bad, but in those days no one thought of taking a photograph of the picture as it was then and of course no one of the group that saw it then remembers at all what it looked like any more than do Picasso or Gertrude Stein.

The Autobiography of Alice B. Toklas,
New York: Harcourt, Brace and Company, 1933

Lionello Venturi

. . . But Picasso's genius was imbued with revolutionary fervor, and the delicacy of the Rose Period was not enough to sustain him. Already in 1906, one can detect something uneasy, something "emancipated" in certain of his portraits, as if a tragic mask was showing through the skin of the model. Then in 1907 *Les Demoiselles d'Avignon* marked the conclusion of a total revolt against tradition, like a manifesto of contempt not only for artistic conventions, but for social ones as well. This intolerance for conformity was not new; in fact, it had already been evident since the time of Impressionism, and even before. But the conventions lasted until the revolt of Picasso, because his was so much more energetic than all the preceding ones. The first ideal that he attacked was that of beauty, which had become an equivocal mask in painting. It was replaced by a tragic grotesqueness, which he sought to establish within ideal geometric forms. Through the centuries, the Renaissance concepts of unity of space by means of perspective had become an ideal more than a scientific principle. When the reduction of space to temporal values, as proposed by Bergson, was put into painting by juxtapositioning, rather than composing the elements of an object, then this ideal seemed mortally wounded.

The renunciation of these two ideals of beauty and spacial positioning contributed in a special way to the creation of Cubism.

In fact, the Cubists dissected the elements of an object, removing from it the very proportion and harmony that is called beauty. They then positioned the elements next to each other in such a way that we would be conscious of their unity in duration rather than in space. And in this way, when they succeeded, they constructed a new relationship between the parts, an equilibrium of succession and stimultaneity that was no longer made up of the parts of an object, but of the parts of a painting. In this respect, they discovered all at once the autonomy of art with respect to nature, and when an observer confronted one of their paintings, they asked that he perceive it as a form created by the imagination, and not as a representation of a natural object. A new beauty then arises from the formal relationships, a new space is born in the world of the imagination, and a new content is conceived in our contemplation of them. Not only Picasso, but also Braque and other painters and poets contributed to the origin of Cubism. But the essential impetus was given by Picasso, who opposed the past to reveal the truth at any cost, even if it was exasperating and ruthless.

Pablo Picasso, catalogue for exhibition
at the Galleria Nazionale d'Arte Moderna, Rome, 1953

Vercors (Jean Bruller)

Then came Picasso. He shattered nature and took upon himself to create a world that no longer consisted of images pilfered from nature, as Rubens or Delacroix had done, but invented images intrinsically belonging to painting, to its texture, to its inherent techniques, in other words an absolutely and uniquely human abstraction. It was the ultimate break. . . . Picasso created a world, a world which breathes and encircles us. A world which revolts and cries out against the abomination of suffering and death, and against those among men who are abject accomplices.

This revolt was much too violent for the great mass of people to have understood immediately its profound munificence, the voice of love which it represents, disguised as mocking desperation. And still today not everyone understands. But to finish I would like to cite an optimistic anecdote. It concerns the time when I was still making my "callichromes," which later . . . I had to abandon. Picasso had entrusted to me for reproduction one of his earlier canvases, an enchanting *Still Life with White Guitar*, delicate in tone. At that time an old electrician who often came to my house was finishing installing electricity in the mill which I had just bought. Watching me work on the picture, he laughingly expressed the common opinion of someone confronting a Picasso canvas: "My grandson could do as well." Then one day a few months later, noticing the little Cubist guitar for the twentieth time, among other works, he became pensive. Turning to my wife, he said with an air of profound wonder: "You can choose not to believe me, Madame, but I am beginning to like that ludicrous Picasso there!" He never knew, of course, what had come over him. But I know. Once his prejudice against a painting that did not imitate reality had fallen, he suddenly felt overwhelmed by the aspiration that lies obscurely in the heart of every human being: the desire to free himself, to refuse submission, and to declare his own independence. His emotion stemmed from having unconsciously and suddenly felt the joy of knowing that he was free, and he realized that he owed this joy to Picasso through the little guitar.

"Pablo the Liberator,"
Europe, Paris, April-May, 1970

Self-Portrait, 1901, on the occasion of Picasso's second visit to Paris

Bibliography

Apollinaire, Guillaume. *The Cubist Painters*. New York: Wittenborn, 1944.

Arnheim, Rudolf. *Picasso's Guernica: The Genesis of a Painting*. Berkeley and Los Angeles: University of California Press, 1962.

Ashton, Dore, ed. *Picasso on Art: A Selection of Views*. New York: Viking, 1972.

Barr, Alfred H., Jr. *Picasso: Fifty Years of His Art*. New York: Museum of Modern Art, 1946.

Blunt, Anthony and Pool, Phoebe. *Picasso: The Formative Years*. Greenwich, Conn: New York Graphic Society, 1962.

Boeck, Wilhelm and Sabartès, Jaime. *Picasso*. New York and Amsterdam: Harry N. Abrams, 1955.

Brassaï. *Picasso & Co*. Garden City, N.Y.: Doubleday, 1966.

Breton, André. *Surrealism and Painting*. New York: Harper and Row, 1973.

Cooper, Douglas. *Picasso Theatre*. New York: Harry N. Abrams, 1967.

Crespelle, Jean-Paul. *Picasso and His Women*. New York: Coward-McCann, 1969.

Czwiklitzer, Christopher, comp. *Picasso's Posters*. New York: Random House, 1970-71.

Daix, Pierre. *Picasso*. New York: Frederick A. Praeger, 1965.

Daix, Pierre and Boudaille, Georges. *Picasso, The Blue and Rose Periods*. Greenwich, Conn.: New York Graphic Society, 1967.

Duncan, David Douglas. *The Private World of Pablo Picasso*. New York: Ridge Press, 1957.

———, ed. *Picasso's Picassos*. New York: Harper & Row, 1961.

Eluard, Paul. *Picasso*. New York: Philosophical Library, 1947.

Gallwitz, Klaus. *Picasso at 90, the Late Work*. New York: G.P. Putnam's Sons, 1971.

Geiser, Bernhard, ed. *Picasso: Fifty-Five Years of His Graphic Work*. New York and Amsterdam: Harry N. Abrams, 1962.

Gilot, Françoise and Lake, Carlton. *Life with Picasso*. New York: New American Library, 1964.

Janis, Harriet and Sidney. *Picasso: The Recent Years: 1939-1946*. Garden City, N.Y.: Doubleday, 1946.

Kahnweiler, Daniel-Henry. *The Rise of Cubism*. New York: Wittenborn, 1949.

———. *The Sculptures of Picasso*. London: Rodney Phillips, 1949.

Kay, Helen. *Picasso's World of Children*. Garden City, N.Y.: Doubleday, 1965.

Leymarie, Jean. *Picasso: The Artist of the Century*. New York: Viking, 1972.

Olivier, Fernande. *Picasso and His Friends*. New York: Appleton-Century, 1965.

Parmelin, Hélène. *Picasso: The Artist and His Model*. New York: Harry N. Abrams, 1965.

Penrose, Roland. *Picasso: His Life and Work*. New York: Harper, 1958.

———. *Portrait of Picasso*. New York: Museum of Modern Art, 1957.

———. *The Sculpture of Picasso*. New York: Museum of Modern Art, 1967.

Penrose, Roland and Golding, John, eds. *Picasso in Retrospect*. New York: Praeger, 1973.

Picasso, Pablo. *Picasso 347*. 2 vols. New York: Random House, 1970.

Picasso. The Arts Council of Great Britain. London: Lund Humphries, 1960.

Richardson, John, ed. *Picasso: An American Tribute*. New York: Chanticleer Press, 1962.

Rubin, William. *Picasso in the Collection of the Museum of Modern Art*. New York: Museum of Modern Art, 1972.

Sabartès, Jaime. *Picasso: An Intimate Portrait*. New York: Prentice-Hall, 1948.

———. *Picasso: documents iconographiques*. Geneva: Pierre Cailler, 1954.

Stein, Gertrude. *Autobiography of Alice B. Toklas*. New York: Harcourt, Brace, 1933.

———. *Picasso*. Boston: Beacon, 1959.

Uhde, Wilhelm. *Picasso and the French Tradition*. New York: Weyhe, 1929.

Vallauris 1954: A Suite of 108 Drawings by Picasso, November 28, 1953 to February 3, 1954. New York: Harcourt, Brace, 1954.

Vallentin, Antonina. *Picasso*. Garden City, N.Y.: Doubleday, 1963.

Vollard, Ambroise. *Recollections of a Picture Dealer*. Boston: Little, Brown, 1936.

Wertenbaker, Lael and the Editors of Time-Life Books. *The World of Picasso, 1881—* New York: Time-Life Books, 1967.

Zervos, Christian. *Pablo Picasso*. 17 vols. Paris: Editions Cahiers d'Art, 1932-66.

Picture Credits

MA is an abbreviation for Mondadori Archives

1 Private collection 2–3 (Edward Quinn) 18 (Budnik-Magnum) 20 (Brassaï) 21 (Cartier-Bresson–Magnum) 23 (MA) 24 top (Grazzini); center (MA) 25 (MA) 26–27 (MA) 28 (MA) 29 top (MA); bottom, Picasso Museum, Barcelona 30 top, Private Collection (MA) bottom (MA) 31 Collection of the Artist 32–33 Picasso Museum, Barcelona and Private Collections (MA) 34 top, Picasso Museum, Barcelona; bottom, Collection of the Artist 35 top and bottom, Chester Dale Collection, National Gallery of Art; center, Nationalmuseum, Stockholm 36 (MA) 37 (MA) 38 (MA) 39 The Art Institute of Chicago 40 (MA) 41 top (Harligue–Viollet); center and bottom (MA) 42 top, Private Collection (MA); left (Brassaï); center (MA); right (Brassaï) 43 left (MA); upper right (MA); bottom right (Collection Viollet) 44 top (Brassaï) center (Cartier-Bresson–Magnum); bottom (Viollet–Remo) 45 (Capa–Magnum) 46 top (Morath–Magnum); bottom left and right (MA) 47 top left (Capa–Magnum); bottom left (MA); right top, center, and bottom (MA) 48–49 (Edward Quinn) 50 left top and bottom (Halsman–Magnum); right top (Marco Mascardi); right bottom (Edward Quinn) 51 (Burri–Magnum) 52 (Carrese) 54–55 Chapel, Vallauris (Ziolo) 57 Private Collections, Stockholm and New York 58 top (Ziolo); bottom, The Solomon R. Guggenheim Museum 59 Private Collection, London (MA) 60 Chester Dale Collection, National Gallery of Art 62 Museum of Modern Art, New York 63 Private Collection (MA) 64 Chester Dale Collection, National Gallery of Art 65 top, Cleveland Museum of Art; bottom, Private Collection, Tokyo 66 Albright-Knox Art Gallery, Buffalo 68 Lillie P. Bliss Bequest, Museum of Modern Art, New York 69 left, Dalzell Hatfield Galleries, Los Angeles (Giraudon); right, Private Collection (Giraudon) 70 The Janis Collection, Museum of Modern Art, New York 71 Private Collection, Zurich (Ziolo) 72 Mrs. Simon Guggenheim Fund, Museum of Modern Art, New York 73 Museum of Modern Art, New York 74 top, Fernand Mourlot, *Art in Posters*, Braziller, New York (MA); center (MA); bottom (MA) 75 (Glinn–Magnum) 76 top (MA); center and bottom left, Lillie P. Bliss Bequest, Museum of Modern Art, New York (MA, Lessing–Magnum); bottom right (Lessing–Magnum) 79 Private Collection (MA) 80 Vallauris (MA) 81 Private Collection (MA) 82 top, Private Collection, Vallauris (Ziolo); bottom (Held-Ziolo) 83 top, Collection of the Artist (Ziolo); bottom, Private Collection (Held-Ziolo) 85 Gallerie Leiris, Paris (MA) 87 top left (Giraudon); bottom left (Hazan); top right, Collection Ramié (Ziolo); below, Private Collection (Giraudon) 88 Chester Dale Collection, National Gallery of Art 89 top (MA); bottom (MA) 90 Collection of the Artist (MA) 93 (MA) 242 Private Collection (MA) 245 Gift of Victor S. Riesenfeld, Museum of Modern Art, New York (MA) 246 (MA) 248 Private Collection 250 top, Private Collection (MA); bottom (MA) 251 (Giraudon) 253 Picasso Museum, Barcelona 255 (MA) 256 Collection of the Artist 257 Museum of Fine Arts, Boston 258 Collection of the Artist (MA) 259 Collection of the Artist (Giraudon) 261 Private Collection 262 Cone Collection, The Baltimore Museum of Art 264 Private Collection

List of Colorplates

INDEX